MW00478331

1. Life Happens
2. My Back Story
3. Trying to Figure Life Out
4. Bethune Cookman Is Where It started
5. Speeding in The Slow Lane
6. What Happened to Me
7. The Great Mistake
8. Work Your Work
9. Half Empty or Hal7f Full
10. Plan your Pursuit
11. Don't Expect Love from Your Hometown
12. Everyone Is Not Going to Like You
13. Be Willing to Sacrifice
14. The Not So Glory Road
15. You Don't Promote You
16. Deal with Bookers the Right Way
17. What Are You Thinking
18. Some Things Must Become an Emergency
19. Commit to Your Commitment
20. Pursue Your Dream Like Your Life Depends On it...Because It does
21. Says Who
22. I've Met Some Cool People
23. Make Your Own Moves
24. Facebook, Family and Funny Comics

Dedications and Thank You

First, I would like to thank God because there is no way I would've ever thought I would write a book in my lifetime. You have blessed me with so many talents and I just want to use every one of them before you call me home. Thank you for not ever giving up on me when I had given up on myself. Thanks for not letting me just lay down and die when I begged you too. I also want to thank my Gunni (Grandmother). I watched you time and time again how you made a way out of no way. You may not have had a lot of money raising us but the lessons you taught us I could never put a price on. Thanks to my mom and dad for being my biggest supporters right now even though neither one of you all wanted to become a comedian. Thanks to Bo, Mikey, Tony, Caree, Candise and momma Debbie for helping me out a lot in life whether it was money, listening, advice or just laughing with me. I love yall. Derrick and Kelsie are my brothers for life. Even when we are wrong at times we never hesitate to tell each other how wrong we were. Not many people have that around them. Trina you and your mom are angels to me and I wouldn't trade you for anything in the world. So glad you found happiness in marriage. Thanks to anyone who allowed me to sleep on their couch on the road to save hotel money, picked me up or gave me a ride, gave me a few dollars to eat or survive, came to a show, booked me or got me booked for a show, told someone about me or a show, purchased anything I was selling, shared my flyers or videos online, messaged me with encouraging words or let me know how a post may have inspired you in some way I want to say Thank You so much. Not many people have the guts to drop everything and pursue what they think is their purpose and I would have never made it to this point without so many people, so much help along the way. Every time I felt like I was about to lose my mind God always placed someone in my life to smooth things out even if only temporary, but I am forever grateful. I wrote this book simply because I had no one to get advice from or any guidance in the comedy game. The established comedians in my city never tried looking out for me or offer any advice so I figured I wouldn't be like them. Everything you will read came from my heart or my experiences I had. Hope you enjoy the read and again thanks for your support.

It's 2017 and I've only been doing comedy almost 8 years. Some may say that I'm not qualified enough to write a book about comedy and its difficulties and its great times. That's why I'm writing about MY LIFE, comedy, the lessons I've learned and the roller coaster of comedy that myself as well as other up and coming comedians must endure.

I am qualified to speak on giving a big part of my life to this. Sacrificing everything from family, money, time, comfort and part of my sanity to pursue what I know is my purpose on this earth at this moment.   I made up my mind not to let comedy, comedians and the business disturb my focus. By limiting my emotional attachment with chaotic situations. I can truly learn and receive the lessons being taught.

Before I get into that I must let you know where I was in life before comedy. I learned that there are 2 very important days in anyone's life. The day you were born and the reason why. A very important thing in your life is that dash in between the start and end date. How would anyone know that you were ever here? What will you leave here on earth besides children and a few unpaid bills?

We all want life to go just as we pictured it when we were thirteen but I'm pretty sure at this point in life you know that's not the case. Many of us spend a great amount of years thinking we were smarter than everyone else. If we did just enough to get by then we would be alright in life. Well my life was no different, but I can be honest and really say that I was not living the life I dreamed of at all. However, in late 2009 I took a great leap of faith not knowing if I would soar or hit rock bottom, but rock bottom was something I was already all too familiar with. The first time I hit rock bottom I was blessed enough to land on my back and that was all I needed because I knew if I can look up I can get up. People fall all the time. Bad things happen to everyone breathing, no one is excluded. The ONLY difference is our thinking and how we choose to handle what has happened. I had a choice to make either I could throw a pity party or refuse to die in my situation.

My entire life I was told to trust in God and pray. That's all I needed. I am now a true believer that God doesn't show us certain paths to life because he knows that 95% won't pursue his purpose for us if we knew what we had to endure and fight through just to get there. I learned why though. Had I known I would be divorced, homeless, car reposed, broke but never broken just so I would learn to not believe in the material things that I took so much pride in having I probably would've begged for another life. I lost almost everything I thought was important, but I never lost my mind.

The most important thing I possess right now today. We are in the greatest times of our lives right now. More opportunities than we've ever had. A tree can only be a tree, a dog can be nothing but a dog but us humans can be anything we truly put our faith, mind and hearts too. I challenge you to stop what you're doing right now and tell yourself what I had to tell myself almost a decade ago. Yesterday I made my last excuse! Every day you make an excuse is a day you put the life you really want to live on the back burner. Make a schedule, start with something as simple as making up the bed every morning.

You may say that's nothing but it's a small accomplishment to start the day. You ever came in the room after a long day to a freshly made up bed? It's a great feeling isn't it. Now write down things you would like to get done daily. Every day may be different. You may have 10 things you would like to get done tomorrow but only get to 8. Isn't that still an accomplishment?

Start your next day doing the things you didn't get too. You must be your own hype man every day. Stop waiting for others to pat you on the back and tell you it's going to okay because it may not ever happen. Once I began depending on making me happy and never depend on anyone else for my happiness something different started happening.

Most people dread Monday mornings because they have to go back to that job that they make so much money at yet hate so much. I'm excited about Monday mornings. It's a new week to get some more things done. I know a few 6-figure people that live vicariously through me. They work, have lots of money but are not enjoying every day like I am. I came to the conclusion that money isn't everything when I learned of millionaires that tried committing suicide.

It's true, we need money to live, but waking up and pursuing your purpose is more gratifying inside and out. Some days you are not going to feel like doing anything, that's when you must get up and do something. Six months from now your life can be completely different if you are willing to give it your all. That's why you can't ever give up. In this book I will tell you about my life and comedy and the lessons I've learned along the way and hopefully show you that success doesn't always makes you happy, but progress does.

1. Life Happens

As soon as I thought I had things figured out life punched me in the face.

Dang 4 a.m. already? Another day at working on 2 and a half hours of sleep. Got in at 1 a.m. from doing what I love just to get some sleep to go do what I hate.

Life is crazy. I promise when I was 24 years old with a college degree I never thought at 34 I would be cutting grass to survive. There was nothing wrong with cutting grass, but for $7.35 a hour it makes it rather frustrating.

Walking around seven hours a day with a weed eater on FIU south campus with a smile on my face just trying not to live in that moment. In life the moment almost doesn't matter as long as you are becoming. I didn't always know this. As long as you are working toward something bigger than your current situation.

I was there physically but, in my head,, I was always onstage with a microphone in hand and anywhere from 5 to 100 strangers sitting in front of me waiting for me to make them laugh. Hell, the only thing that kept me sane was thinking about the stage.

Fresh from divorce, checks were about $350 after working 80 hours. Child support don't have no love let's just say. This was my routine about 4 days a week every week for almost 2 years. When I wasn't onstage I would do anything, and I mean anything to keep my mind off my current situation, so depression wouldn't set in which it often did.

The only thing that made me happy at this point was the love I received from total strangers at shows. The laughs and applause said man we love you, keep on keeping on. I was in love with that feeling. I wasn't making any money, but I didn't care, I just wanted the people who were showing me love to never leave. I didn't want to go face my real life just, yet which eventually led to sleeping on porches, in my truck or on someone's couch. I was throwing rocks at the jailhouse night in and night out driving sometimes up to an hour and a half for 5 minutes of stage time with suspended license. Leaving open mics driving back home after midnight leaving me to be the only car on the road sometimes being a big target for police. I was really in no rush to get anywhere after shows though mainly because i really had no place to go.

I would stay with women that I really didn't like just to lay in a bed for a night. Yep, that was me. The guy that just rocked the club, stayed and shook everyone's hand and was asked to take pics with people yes, homeless. Don't get me wrong I'm sure someone in my family would've let me stay with them for a while but if you know me I hate feeling like I'm a burden on anyone. Pride had me messed up for a while. If I had to do it over again I would tell pride to go to hell. When the only people you feel understands you are drug attics and you're not even on drugs made me feel some type of way.

I told no one my situation and I moved around so much that no one probably even noticed. Every day was a mental fight for me. I didn't ever remember waking up one single day in my life and saying to myself "I want to eventually be homeless one day" but I was knee deep in it. I was so depressed with my life I had darn near became an alcoholic overnight.

That wasn't my goal, that's not anyone's goal in life, but it happens. One thing about being an entertainer we all suffer from some type of demon. I had played around with good people and took them for granted. God blessed me to have way too many good people in my life and still doing so. I thought I had all the sense though, I knew everything except what I needed to know. A man that knows something knows that he knows nothing.

I had played around with life so long that it finally ran me down. I remember for at least a month waking up wherever I was at the time and asking God why does he keep waking me up just let me die in my sleep but God never would kill me. I was upset. The turtle always catches up with the rabbit eventually I guess. Didn't break me though. God kept saying I won't let you off the hook that easy so either get off your butt and live or die in misery. Walk with me.

2. My Back Story

Life! It's never all bad but it's never all good either

I don't remember too much about my childhood, so I will share with you what I can remember. I grew up in Miami in a neighborhood called Richmond Heights. It wasn't the best neighborhood, but it wasn't the worse either. The one thing I love about the neighborhood was we all were like family. No matter what area of the neighborhood the graveyard, power plant, Van Buren, the four-way, new section we all knew each other and showed love. I got the nickname Spunky at a real early age. Maybe about 3 I think. My mother says she use to take me to some department store and soon as we stepped in the door I would run to this pregnant lady behind the counter, lift up her dress and rub her stomach for as long as she allowed me too. That's it people, that's how I got the name Spunky. No real awesome story behind it. My mom kept me and my brother Tony in almost every sport that Richmond Park had. Tony is my big little brother.

Super talented guy he just never really got a full grip on life, but you couldn't tell him that. Super smart guy though. One thing about him is that he could make anybody laugh at any moment. I tell people I work to be funny, he's light years funnier than I am without even trying. I also have two other brothers and two sisters from my dad. Bo (Charles) He's my oldest brother. Military. He is always in chill mode, sort of like he never wanted any problems he just wanted to live a little. It's funny because he lives a pretty dope life that I never figured out. He supports me from far but I know if I really needed him he wouldn't hesitate to be there. Then there's Michael. He's the youngest out of us all and clearly have the most swag. He's a product of the social media era and he take full advantage of it. Cool kid who joined the military shortly after high school. His thing is shoes. I've never seen anyone with as many pairs of shoes as he has. No kids, no girlfriend I guess he needed something to spend all that military money on. Our dad has these false hopes that he's getting married any day now. None of the other kids actually believe it when our dad says it. I don't even believe his own mother believes it.

Shacaree is the oldest sister. She was my closest out of all the others besides Tony for a while. I'm guessing because we were so close in age. We can talk and listen to each other's messed up relationship stories and make jokes out of it. Of course, I had way more horror stories than her. Candise, my baby sister is the queen B of us all. No matter where we go she would get all the attention. She wasn't loud she is just cute as they come. Hell, we all are. Me more than the rest but you get the picture. Candise is probably the nicest meanest person you will meet but if she's down with you then she's all the way down. You must love that about a woman. We all didn't grow up together but today you couldn't tell. We get together and it's none stop foolishness. Always fun times. Problem is we are rarely together because of our busy lives. My dad made sure when we got old enough that we knew who each other were. I used to question why we didn't live with my daddy but when you get married and have kids of your own you understand that life happens. You begin to wonder all types of things like was my mom one of those women and kept us from him? Did my dad move on with his new wife and new family and figured he'd come back when the smoke was clear? Sometimes when children are involved a lot of spiteful things are done on both parents and by the time you hear everyone's truth it doesn't even matter anymore. Funny part is once I got old enough I didn't care about that. All I cared about was our current relationship. I'm not the one to make an excuse about how my life turned out because of who was or wasn't around. I figured it's best to take full advantage of our time left with each other. One thing I do know is that my mom and Gunni (Grandmother) tried their very best when it came to raising me and Tony and that's all we could ask. With me being the youngest in my grandma's house when she scraped her money together to buy as much Popeyes chicken that she can afford I was often left with little to nothing to eat. Many days I would eat cream corn straight out the can in private, so I wouldn't complain to my grandma who I knew was trying her very best. One thing I did do was dress really nice in high school but that was thanks to my auntie Tara. Nope she didn't buy us clothes I would wait until she left for work every morning and break in her room and pick my outfit for the day and get home early enough to hang them back up before she got home. I was in high school wearing all these bright colors and folks thought I was just different when in fact they were my aunt Tara's clothes. Highschool is where I learned how to hustle. If I wasn't shooting dice I was playing team spades for money and stacking the deck when it was my turn to deal so I would always win. I also played tonk mostly and would always find a way to cheat. Most days were all about gambling. How I passed classes is still a mystery. I used to say "I gamble for bread and meat so if I don't win I won't eat." I knew most of the time my mom and Gunni didn't have it, so I wouldn't even ask for lunch money. I know all too well the feeling of your child asking you for a few dollars day in and out and you never have it. It's not a good feeling at all. Having children of my own made me realize that there is no manual for raising your kids. Just do the best that you can. Nobody wants their child to experience some of the tough times they had to deal with and that's fine, but those hard times is what made us aren't they. It made us tough, taught us how to endure hard times keep the faith and just keep pushing.

We didn't spend a lot of time with my dad's side of the family growing up, but I do remember my dad bringing me and my brother over some super fresh University of Miami jackets one Christmas. I remember that in particular because me and my brother was happy, and my mom wasn't it seemed. I didn't understand. I didn't want to. This came from my dad that's all that mattered. I found out in 2016 that the entire time he had been paying child support. The amount I don't know but at least it was something. I will tell you why I say that later. I'm not sure that there is a sport that I can't play and be competitive at it. We played everything. Not just me and my brother but all of our friends. My dad told me he was there at most games but never said anything to us because of whatever situation he and my mother must've been going through. I completely understand now. I wish he would've though. I was always a good athlete but an average student. I wasn't dumb at all I just always did enough to pass. Today I get so upset with my own children for being just like me. Crazy huh. I was never really shy growing up. I specifically remember me acting crazy on the school bus once and the bus driver let me get off the bus, called me back over and said "You always acting crazy every day. You ain't nothing but a dang comedian." Never once in the next 20-year span that I ever thought she was telling the truth. Crazy thing is I saw her right after I started in 2010 at a club and she remembered me and asked me to walk her to her car. She looked nice and I was feeling myself, so I agreed. We walked slow because she was in these really high heels that was hurting her feet and I was feeling tipsy.

Her: What are you doing with your life?

Me: I'm a comedian now.

Her: Boy quit playin.

Me: Nope. I remember you telling me I should be a comedian.

Her: I sure did. I remember. Okay well let me know where you gone be at, so I can come check you out.

Funny thing about what she said which I didn't know is that 85% of the people you talk to about shows would tell you that. They would basically tell you that bold face lies as a way to have conversation. I call it empty convo. This conversation really isn't going anywhere. Many, if not all entertainers go through that at some point. All of a sudden, we reached her car and she opens the door, stands in the door of her car, squat down and starts pissing right there. People walking right by. That didn't bother me too much. What bothered me was she never stopped talking while she was peeing. I think I only remember that night because she told me I should be a comedian first. My mother always said she thinks I will be a pastor. Though she's probably disappointed that I'm not in the pulpit she still encourages me not to ever give up.

3. Trying to Figure Life Out

Sometimes when it's time to grow up life doesn't make an announcement it forces its way on you

I can honestly say I've done so much in my lifetime. I've learned lessons that I teach my kids and anyone else who would listen. Most people who know me from my earlier days knows that I used to be a dancer. Not a stripper but a dancer. Back in the early 90s in Miami that was the thing. Everybody wanted to dance and be in a dance group. Even the thugs secretly wanted to dance. They would never say so but catch them at a party and let their song come on they would turn the party out. We mainly just competed with other dance groups in the city. We rarely got paid anything, but we just wanted to compete with the other groups in Miami and be talked about. Of course, groups like Splack Pack and No Good but So Good were out of our league but we didn't care. We were a bunch of young cocky dudes who was out to prove something. We could dance too. Our reward was all the women we would get after the shows. That's all that mattered. Girls! Our name was the Kool aid pack. Jeff, Cooley, Sam, Lil Dee, Andre and Lucious. We were hot in our area which was right up our alley because all we wanted was attention from the women. Dancing brought me my first older woman and eventually first-born child. I remember we did a show in Homestead, FL and as soon as we walked in I saw the finest girl I had seen in a while. Nice shape, pretty smile. Okay it was really this girl Toya that was about 5 years older than me that I had been seeing around the neighborhood that would never give me the time of day. Thing is she didn't know I danced so when she saw me walk in with all my homies she looked shocked. At that moment I knew that night was my big chance to impress her. I was backstage telling all the other dancers about her and how I will out dance them all to get her attention. We were basically brothers, so it was always a competition. I danced like I never danced before. We lost that contest to a group name Get It From The Back only because they had this guy Rashad who could dance like you've never seen. Dude was literally a one man show and usually got all the women we wanted. Well actually they lost, and I won. The very next morning my mom came and woke me up about 10 a.m. She said, "aye boy, it's some girl at the door". A girl came to my house. Oh shoot. I don't even think I brushed my teeth I was so excited. I went to the door and when I opened it there was Toya. I didn't even know she knew where I lived. I was too excited. We talked for a little while and then she left but we agreed to meet up later that evening. We chilled at a party and ended up keeping in touch with each other. Toya and I were cool together. She had children already which was cool. What I didn't know was her and her children's father was in this crazy off and on relationship. I didn't care though, I had Toya paying attention to me. Shortly after we started really chilling together I made a decision to join the military. Yep, U.S. Navy folks. I just wanted to do something different. I hated high school so college was out of the question. Great Lakes Illinois was where boot camp was. I knew boot camp wouldn't be hard because I was always an athlete. Hardest part was leaving my girlfriend Toya. I was so head over heels. I think because I was dating an older woman. My mom would always ask her "what do you want with my baby" and Toya would just smile and say, "I don't know." I didn't know either, hell I didn't care. Okay here's the plan, I go to the military, make some money then me and Toya live happily ever after with her 2 boys. That plan went out the door 3 days into boot camp. I get there, and we can't use the phone. Wait I can't call my mom or Toya? Well send me home. That's stupid, that's not fair I don't want to be here! How can I go back home sir? NO! Okay I will show you. I then found out that being rebellious in boot camp is not the smartest thing. I realize that in the middle of trying to make the roof sweat. If you've been in the Navy you probably know what I'm talking about. Later that night I cried because I didn't want to be there.

Bunkmate: Aye you really want to get out?

Me: Heck yeah man this is stupid.

Bunk mate: I may have a way but you may not like it.

Me: Tell me it's done.

Bunkmate: You gotta act gay or make them think you have   a mental problem.

Me: Yeah, I will just act crazy.

Long story short a week later I got cleared to get out. I was not kissing no man just to leave but I did run circles around the psychologist and made him think I wanted to kill myself and him. Still to this day I wish I would've stayed in boot camp. I went home and did everything wrong. Sold drugs, getting shot at, crackheads stealing from me, getting robbed, needless to say it was bad. I had friends whose house I would go over during the day. Me, Derrick and Kelsie would play video games all day and I would sell drugs all night. Their sister Trina was a bit older, so she was off doing her own thing, but you didn't want to make her mad. Anyways this was my new little family that I was around the most. I was living a double life, and nobody knew except Derrick and Kelsie. I covered the fact that I always had money by working at Popeyes part time. One day after I had gotten shot at running from the robbers, their mom Ms. Emma G. Lordeus came to me and told me I can no longer be in Miami. She said she knew I didn't like school, but I won't be alive if I stayed in Miami. I think Derrick snitched on me to his mom. She ended up being my angel. She was so right but I really didn't want to leave Miami. Either way it was the best thing to ever happen to me. She literally saved my life. I'd probably not be alive or would've been in prison somewhere had she not done what she did for me. She did all my paperwork for college, bought me a plane ticket and sent Derrick and I to Defiance College. Everything about that idea was great except for the fact that I had to leave my girl Toya AGAIN. At that point we were up and down. She would kick me out about twice a month and then her mom would call me and tell me to come back. We were crazy. Not to mention she was pregnant. I had to go try to do something with my life. While at Defiance College, I played football and ran track and was good at both but there was only one big problem. There was only one black girl in the entire school. I had never seen that before. I didn't even know it was possible at the time. No way I'm staying here. I thought, how can I get out of here and where can I go? Then, I got a call on October 18, 1996; Toya said she had my first child.

I was so happy but felt so bad that I wasn't there to see him. What was even worse is that I couldn't afford to go home and meet my son. I had to wait until winter break which was 2 months later. No worries. I was just glad I had my son. We fussed that he wasn't named after me but she had already had a son with my first name, so it made sense not to have two sons with the exact same name. I was just being stupid. I knew I couldn't stay in Ohio with a son so me and Derrick decided to transfer to Bethune Cookman College in Daytona Beach. I was closer to my son and would be around some people that looked like me, dressed like me, talked like me, and I was in heaven looking at all the beautiful women every day. This was enough for me to keep going. I don't think I've ever been to any classes that much in my life.

4. Bethune Cookman Is where It Started

Knowing what you don't want in life is just as important as knowing what you do want

I've roasted a lot in high school at Miami Killian. We would gamble at lunch and whoever would lose would roast everybody he could see, to keep from showing he was bothered from losing. At Bethune Cookman, there was no mercy. I was so close to never even making it to Bethune. The day before I was to leave for college, I was out early in the morning in Miami selling drugs, so I wouldn't go to college broke. I was out there alone so I had a stash spot not too far away from me, so I wouldn't have drugs on me. I was making a sale and passing by at the same time was a community control car. I really didn't think anything about it because we really didn't take those people serious. I went on about my day and the community control car shows up again across the street. Shortly after a real police car pulls up next to them and they started talking. I knew I had to get out of there now. Soon as I made a move to leave they both pulled up on me. What saved me was after my last sale, I never put the drugs back in my stash spot. I had them in my hand. The police call me to his car while the community control officer goes exactly to my stash spot looking for my drugs. This was in 1997 so we still had real portable cd players still. I'm standing outside the officer's door as he stood inside the doorway. He's asking me all my info, so he could check my name for warrants. At this time, I'm standing in the police face with a hand full of drugs that would've easily sent me away for a few years. I was bobbing my head as if I was really listening to music but instead I slightly popped the cd player open a slid the drugs in the cd player. At this point I'm scared out of my mind but I knew I can't make a mistake or this officer was about to be in a track meet because I was going to run. It came back I had no warrants so he told me to leave and not come back that day. I jumped on my bike and nearly fell trying to get away so fast. I still have the scar on my leg from when I missed the pedal and scratched it because

I was so afraid. On my way home, I must've thanked God fifty times for getting me out of that. I stayed in the house for the rest of the day and was ready to get out of Miami and get to college. I had never been to Daytona Beach before, but I've always heard about how fun it was at black college reunion. From the very first day I got to Daytona Beach I was in love with college. I will be the first person to tell anyone I don't care what college you attended, nothing is better than a HBCU. I played cornerback on the football team and every road trip at dinner, two offensive lineman Shawn Banks and Goldiee would roast the entire team and dared anyone to roast back. A few of us tried it with very little success. This went on for the 2 years I played and even years after we graduated. Shawn and Goldiee would call me 3 way and the minute they heard my voice they would take turns roasting me until I fought back. This would happen like clockwork for the first 10 minutes of every call and then we would have a conversation afterwards. And most of the times it went like this.

Goldiee: Spunk man go head and be a

comedian.

> Me: Nah man I'm good

> Goldiee: See how you roast with us. Just translate that to   the stage.

> Me: Nah man that's y'all.

> Shawn: Man get yo' scary butt onstage and quit playing.

> Me: Man shut up Shawn I'm no comedian.

> Goldiee: Dog you're funny at least try it.

> Shawn: You know if that receiver takes you deep and score a touchdown you got to still go back on the field the next series and redeem yours. Same thing with comedy chump, if you bomb then get right back on stage and find a way to win.

Strange but they knew that talking in football terms would get me to understand that it's just like comedy in a way. It actually worked though. This same convo went on for years. I didn't ever want to be a comedian. I just wanted to play arena football and have fun with life. Though I never desired to be a comic I had always looked at all the Def Comedy Jam and Comic View episodes countless amounts of times but to actually do it myself was never a thought. I had a lot going on. A little too much. Enough for me to lay down and quit but I just never gave up on what could be. Funny thing is now that I am a comedian makes Bethune-Cookman with four professional comedians that are alumni but for some reason they won't book any of us except Rod Z to perform at homecoming or any other events. Shrugs.

While at Bethune I met some of the coolest people. We were all like a small fraternity that had our own little hustles. Our house was basically the money house and the college students knew it. If you wanted a shot to make money, then you could come to our house almost any time of the day and get a shot at some money. We had a few different houses that we lived in, but it was always Me, Derrick, Sam Bo and Greg King. We eventually moved on Oak street in Daytona Beach and that's when a lot changed. My cousin Curt came over more often and he brought his homies with him. Phil, Mike, the twins, Cee Lo, Twan, and D Real. Also, at this time my brother Tony had moved up to Daytona and eventually invited Ollie Parker up for black college weekend, but he never left. I kind of wish I would've made him go back to Miami though. Maybe he wouldn't be appealing a life sentence right now. Everybody had a hustle, but Derrick was the only one in the entire house who actually did something legal. Mostly all of us were full time students. Everyone else was betting on video football games, shooting dice, credit card scams, sold drugs or street raced. Every Thursday Curt and a few others would get people from around the city and sometimes state to come and we would run for whatever amount they wanted to bet. Everyone around us had money so the bets were always covered. Besides, we knew no one could beat us running on feet so we were never worried about losing. I remember I was at this telemarketing job I had just gotten to start my scam, which would later get me arrested and I get a phone call that the 100-meter champion in the state of Georgia wanted to race me. At this point I had never lost a street race ever. Curt told me it's big money out there and they won't wait for me to get off work, so I faked like I was sick and got off work. Soon as I pulled on "the Ave" it's kaotic. People are everywhere. I parked my car in the girl's dorm and went to find my boys. I get to them and somethings wrong. My boy D Real was saying some guys were talking smack to him. I knew this wasn't good because he was a fighter. Him, Mike and Sam together were never good. I tell them I'm going to the house to get the rest of the guys don't move I'm coming right back. I go to my car and pull around the Ave and before I knew it D real is in the middle of the street fighting. Heck I think everyone was fighting. I sped up and stopped right in front of the fight. Everything slowed down. I watched a guy slowly walk in the middle of the chaos, points a gun to the back of D reals head and pull the trigger. Boom! The guy turns and walks off like he didn't just shoot someone. Sam ran and grabbed D Reals arm and drug him out the street. Right then I hit the gas going to tell the other guys. I knew he had to be dead by the way he dropped. Everybody jumped in my car and some ran over but by the time we got back he was deceased. Just like that. It was like a bad dream. Shortly after, I left Bethune my senior season, to go try out for the Georgia Force arena football team in Atlanta. My cousin Tommy drove with me. We must've had $100 between the both of us for gas and food. Tryouts are over, and we knew we didn't have enough gas or money to make it to Miami, so we came up with this bright idea that if we left at night then we would burn less gas. I'm not sure who's smart idea that was. We were going through Valdosta Georgia and I knew if we could just get to Daytona I could borrow money to get us home. Well I was unaware I was speeding and got pulled over. I had license and so did he, so there were no worries. I told Tommy "aye man this guy is taking a long time to come back." Then another police car shows up. Anyone in an urban neighborhood knows when another officer shows up that's not good. I noticed when he got out of his car he put my license in his front pocket. Now I'm confused, I know my license are good. He said, "hey man You have a warrant in Daytona Beach." Right then I knew what it was. I had a fraud warrant from scamming a crazy amount of credit cards from people who rarely used their USAA credit cards. How the heck did I forget about that? Month earlier the police detective called my phone wanting to talk to me before, but I told them talk to me when you catch me. I knew I had a decent alibi being that it was so much traffic in our house and only 2 of us had cell phones the scam could've been ran by anyone using my phone. I told my cousin just to get to Daytona and he should be good. I told him to tell them to get me out of jail asap. I'm in jail in Valdosta, Georgia and the people were cool for the most part. I'm guessing because I gave away my meals because I just knew I wasn't going to be in there long. That lasted about three days. Everyone was asking me what I in there for was, but I wouldn't tell them. Day 4, day 5, I couldn't believe I was still in there. Someone said hey man good news is if they don't expedite you in ten days then they have to release you. Okay so I'm hoping these next 5 days go by quickly. Day 7, day 8, the morning of day 9 they came to get me. I was so upset. I rode in the back of a sheriff's car handcuffed from Valdosta to Daytona. That was a low point in my life, but I knew if I get to Daytona I could get out. I got there, and I spoke to my brother if I recall and I told them to gather $20 from everyone in the house and my girlfriend will drive from Miami with the rest to get me out. Short story short, no one gave me a dime. I was disappointed being that I had looked out for so many of them and I knew they were all getting money. I eventually pled out to 3 years' probation and pay the restitution and a load of community service hours. It was cool because I knew I really didn't get in trouble I just made a mistake. My girlfriend who eventually became my wife drove pregnant in the middle of the night and bailed me out and we drove straight back to Miami. I didn't want to even see those guys. The next 2 times I went to jail was for refusing a DUI breathalyzer test. In the hood, people tell you to never blow but, no one tells the rest of the story. When you refuse it automatically suspends your license for a year the 1st time. The second time for 5 years. I refused twice in a two-year span which cost me close to fifteen thousand dollars total to get my driver's license back. No one tells you that if you refuse to have a lot of money because it's going to cost you. The smarter thing is to blow and take your charge, get a lawyer, then get it reduced to a reckless driving. It cost me a lot of money to learn that lesson.

5. Speeding in The Slow Lane

Sometimes we are so smart that we are dumb

The one thing I can actually sit down and say is, I shouldn't have ever gotten married. Okay getting married so young was a bad move for ME. She was my sister's college roommate. So, when my sister would come see me, her roommate would come. In college, I was kind of THAT guy. I saw her. She had this big old butt and the smallest waist line. A little cutie. We exchanged emails and kept in touch. I joke with my sister all the time that I shouldn't have never opened that email.   We were not really ready. I know I wasn't. I was still playing arena football and she had graduated college, so she moved in with me until I finished college also. In the midst of all this she had gotten pregnant. Lord knows I didn't want another child at that point. Hell, I could barely help take care of my oldest son Khamari, even though I was seeing a few dollars. But, it was her first child and I couldn't have her make that decision, so we decided to have the baby. Well I really had no choice actually. She was ready to start her life and family so that's what we tried to do. We moved with a few family members in Miami and I remember being at the Flea Market Mall when I bought her a ring and decided to propose to her over a nice spaghetti dinner. On the day we got married I should've known it was going to be a long ride when he said, "you may now kiss the bride" and she started laughing. I still don't know why she laughed. I just know for the next few years there was very few to laugh about. I tell people she wasn't a bad wife at all she was just not a good one for ME. Doesn't make her bad. We both did things and that's it. It wasn't all bad actually and I learned a few really great lessons. What I did learn was that no matter how long you've been knowing someone you never really truly know someone. I learned the do's and don'ts in a marriage vs. a relationship and listen to those that's closest to you. No one wanted me to marry her, so I did. Hell, I'm sure no one wanted her marrying me either. But that's what we did. Everything went so fast though. Baby, married, house, job, career. Things were going good for the most part until she made a mistake. Fast forward a little. I'm not completely sure where I was in life, but I do know that I wasn't in a good place. I ran a small lawn care business, so I would sleep later than her. She was a teacher. A great one. I also eventually became a teacher of Social Studies and Life Management also, but I was nowhere near as good as she was at teaching. She was on her email one morning conversing with a guy she dated in college. The mistake was she must've been in a rush because she never logged out of the email so when I got up to use the computer the email popped up. I read it and it basically was saying how she wanted one more weekend with him and they were planning it at that point. I never lost my cool, but I printed out the email to give to her and then I emailed him back and told him he could have her when she came for the weekend. He emailed back saying I'm gonna lose a good woman blah blah blah. I said, "oh you mean the woman who's married and trying to sleep with you, that good woman." He never responded. When she got home she laid in the bed. I asked about her day and then laid the email on her chest and walked away. She jumped out the bed yelling and screaming but it all fell on deaf ears at that point. I just knew she had woken up a bear and nothing would be the same.

The next few years consisted of me having numerous women, numerous jobs, and partying and living like I was single. Coming in the house the next morning and didn't care whether I stayed married or not. In my mind the one thing I was totally against (marriage) she ruined it by trying to step out. I know the only thing that stopped her was the fact that she got caught. Hell, she may've still went through with it for all I know, but I didn't care. Now that I look back on the situation I should've went about things totally different. I never gave her any opportunity to speak on it. I was young and just went with what I knew. As men we are expected to be something that we never see. We never had an example in front of us to show us how to go about things the right way when you grow up without a man around. My grandfather did his own thing, most of my uncles and cousins were gangsters and criminals. Even my mom's boyfriend was in the streets so that's what I was around the most. So now we have 2 kids, our son together and I now have custody of my oldest child when his mother decided she wanted to get out of Miami. I didn't blame her. Though she made pretty good money, Miami is hard to survive with only one income and kids to feed. I didn't care about her leaving. She and I always been cool for the most part and she needed a breath of fresh air from Miami, so I was happy for her. Besides she left my son with me and my wife, so it was cool. My son moving in with us slowed my life down a little from this selfish rampage I was on. I didn't party as much but when I didn't I just would sit in the rocking chair watching t.v. with a drink like I was a true alcoholic, but I wasn't, I was just miserable. So much happen in the next few years that I still get irritated thinking about it. If I can be honest I can say one thing I hated most was that my opinion wasn't good enough until her aunt or mother said it was good. Nothing wrong with a second opinion but about everything was just stupid to me. My opinion alone was never good enough until someone in her family said it was cool. One thing I appreciated was her aunt Vanessa and uncle James Faulk were true human beings. They didn't take sides and if you were wrong then that's just that. They alone helped save my butt several times and did what they could to keep our head above water. During my struggle we had a daughter. Auntie Vanessa and Uncle James were like angels when it came to all of us. I love those two, but I was trying to be a man about the situations we got in, so I would try not to run to them for much even though I should've. My family lived on the south end of Miami, so I was basically all alone against her family most of the time. Crazy part is if I really had started talking about some of the things that happened between some of her family and friends then everyone would've been mad, but I don't like conflict, so I'd shut up. When things were falling apart I saw how fast people would turn on you soon as they see an opportunity. I knew the end was coming I just didn't know when. A person can only take so much, especially women. I knew exactly what I was doing though. The way we thought and grew up was different and it took years for me to figure out why she thought a certain way. She didn't grow up rich, but her family still managed to sort of spoil her. Rightfully so, she was the baby girl.

Spoiled so much that her nickname was "Money." I thought it was cute at first and I enjoyed calling her that until I really realized why she had the name. My family on the other hand weren't close to being well off either. Hell, I was born with nothing, and I still have most of it left. There was no one to pick us up when we fell so we basically had to figure out how to win, rely on our ability and faith. We learned not to fold, and fight through things. I'm not saying she wasn't, but we would deal with hard times very differently. She would often panic, and I would think hey I've been here before let's keep it moving. I wasn't aware at that time that a lot of women are concerned with what others think about them and how it looks to others. I didn't. I rarely cared about much. My mom and my oldest son's mom would always tell me that I was so nonchalant about everything in life. I hadn't even realized it, but it was so true. It's sad to say but the struggle had become normal for me. Like a part of my day but I had no time to ever feel sorry for myself. I knew there was no one to come save me. I just continued telling myself, just don't give up something good will happen eventually and it did, eventually.

6. What Happened to me

It's not about who's right or wrong but simply what's right or wrong

I can honestly say I can look past almost anything. When it comes to kids, especially mine I can't so much. Before I get into this I must say my ex-wife was a blessing by helping me raise and take care of my oldest son Khamari. I'm so grateful for everything she's done for him but in a snap of a finger she switched up on him because of our beef. I learned to not ever put anything past anyone. Even if she is your wife. By no means don't think I'm about to go on this bash your ex-wife spree. Nope! I'm just going to tell my truth as I seen it. Keep in mind we were young, I was probably still very immature, so I was no angel by any stretch of imagination at this point.

I've always been the person to tell people if you have an issue with someone then don't take it out on anything else but that person. Not their pets, their cars, their friends nor their family. So, at this point we are at our worse probably. Things changed and changed quickly. She began taking my younger son somewhere else to get his haircut instead of letting me take him to the barber we had been going to for years. It literally took a few haircuts to notice that. I thought maybe she just got his haircut while she was out. Turns out his barber would be her boyfriend. I even went to pay him for my son's haircut once. Shook his hand and all. She started not coming home after work until eight, nine and sometimes ten p.m. This was sort of a problem because she had our little kids with her, but I had my oldest at home with me. The problem was I didn't know how to cook so I would have to call my grandma or mother and ask how to cook rice and spaghetti and different meats just so there would be food ready when everyone got home because they were getting in so late. Problem was my little ones would come in take a bath then go to bed. This went on for weeks. I didn't mind because I didn't want to be around her anyway. Things had gotten so bad that when she did come in early, my son Khamari and I would go sit in my truck and watch movies until he fell asleep. I can tell he didn't like being in that house either. Most of what was going on was probably my fault, but I was so stubborn that I didn't even see it. One day me and the boys were riding in Liberty City and jokingly I asked my youngest son, "AJ why y'all never eat daddy cooking when y'all come home? Y'all don't like my food." He then said something that would change everything. He said, "no dad we go to TT Vanessa house or granny house after school and eat before we come home." Oh ok. Wait! So she knows I can't cook so she was not coming home to cook for Khamari on purpose. It was a Thursday. I remember it like yesterday because by Friday morning I withdrew Khamari from school, transferred him to another school, and moved him in with my mother down south. I continued to stay in the house with the other kids because they were small, and I never ever wanted them to constantly wake up and daddy wasn't around. I slept in their room on a twin bed and they slept in the bed with her with the door locked. We walked right past each other on a daily basis like we were the wallpaper. It was horrible. She would text my phone out the blue with full conversations about me and while I'm reading it she would text again "my bad that text wasn't meant for you." That must've happened fifty times. I actually tell that joke today. I always thought either she's not that bright or she's doing it on purpose. At that point it didn't even matter. Now my son Khamari was in a better living condition and I could concentrate on other things though. I tried to right my wrongs, tried to pray together, I even suggested counseling which I don't even believe in. Nothing worked. As a matter of fact, it had gotten worse. I guess all the wild living made her fed up. One day I was at my friends Tameka Sweat and Henry's house. Sweat and I went to college together and was always cool. She was like one of the fellas when it came to talking because I would go and talk to them and make jokes about my miserable life. She and Henry seemed to have it all together and living a happy life. I just wanted to be around happy people. They never judged me just mainly laughed. She had her mom there that heard our convo day in and day out and she asked, "hey how old are you? 29? Man, you are still young. You are handsome and educated. You can start a new life man. See I'm in my 50's, I'm stuck in my ways but if you living with someone you shouldn't be walking round no house not talking to each other like y'all the damn wallpaper. Get Out now! People think they are doing their kids a favor by staying around but kids notice more than what we think!" They knew we were at odds and I was being selfish staying in that unhealthy situation. As much as the thought of me leaving bothered me, she was absolutely right. I always told myself she'd come around eventually we, have kids together. At this point I knew our time had ran its course. I went home and sat at the kitchen table for almost an hour thinking about if I made this move how life would change big time. I thought long and hard for at least two hours and then I threw a small candle against the wall and broke the glass as to say I'm doing it, I'm leaving. She came out the room so fast as if she was standing at the door waiting for me to do something crazy. She left and came back with her uncle and the police. I was laughing because I'm the most non-threatening guy on earth but if you know her you know she's the biggest drama queen God created. The police made me pack some things to leave for the night. I was happy to leave even if it was by force but then she said something that I didn't want to even believe. I'm packing and putting stuff in my truck and she just yells "you're damn right I wasn't feeding your kid, he ain't mine." I couldn't believe it. I looked at her uncle and he dropped his head because he knew how messed up that was to say. Shortly after I left basically started my stint of being in a homeless situation. I left with no plan. It didn't matter because I was away from her. In the bible it says a man would rather sleep on the roof of the house than in the house with a nagging woman. This was so true in my case. I would rather sleep on the street or in my truck than in the same house with her. I think no one should live like that ever. It's painful. There's not many things that we get only one of, and life is the most important thing, so I refuse to ever live it unhappily. The next few years consisted of me sleeping on people's floors, couches, in my truck until that got reposed, on someone's porch or in an after-hour club. I use to wake up every day for months and ask God why is he keeping me alive. I couldn't do anything for myself or my kids so why am I alive please just let me die. This went on for a long time until I realized God wasn't going to give me the easy way out of life and allow me to die so I had to do something, anything. I was so close to giving up. Then I found out my messed-up life was pretty funny to people. My sister Trina allowed me to sleep on her couch for a while and did her very best to make me as comfortable as a 30-year-old healthy man could be. She never asked for anything even though I know she needed help a lot of times considering she had 5 kids in the house she had to provide for on whatever the school bus system paid. Her mom saved my life back in 1997 and here she is picking up where her mom left off. We all go through rough times in life. I never wanted people to feel sorry for me I just wanted to figure out how can I get past these tough times and quit being a liability to people.

7. The Great Mistake

Sometimes you don't choose the life you live, it chooses you

Coming in to comedy one would think that since we are a community of people that brings joy to others that we would be happy and cool right? Wrong! I've met some of the most angriest people on the planet that are comedians. Now I will take you back to how I mistakenly got into comedy.

2009, I was hearing about a new comedy show they were starting. I was excited because since I was young I loved comedy, never wanted to be a comedian but I love to laugh. I would ride the city bus every single Thursday and lie and tell the door girl and security I was a comic because I didn't have ten dollars to pay to get in. My third show attending I met one of the nicest comedians ever, Barbara Carlyle. We talked a little about comedy then she gave me her number and told me to call her if I wanted advice. She didn't even realize I wasn't a comedian. I could've sworn she liked me that night. I was excited because I had seen her on television and was happy I talked to her. She's the first comedian that I've ever seen on television in my life, so I was too excited. I told everybody about her like I was the man. Few weeks passed and I'm back in there watching another comedian I had saw on television, but this comedian was bombing badly. I mean badly. It was weird because I knew how funny he was on t.v. years back. I felt bad for him. Miami crowds are tough, even to this day. People are just angry. You ever heard someone say if you can make it here you can make it anywhere, that's Miami. It's combat comedy in south Florida. I asked Larry, "hey he's getting paid for this" he said, "yes fifteen hundred dollars, if I didn't pay him already he would be in trouble." He laughed but I always wondered was he dead serious. I said "fifteen hundred? I can do that for fifteen hundred dollars." I thought all comedians got paid like that. I was so wrong. I went and sat on the porch and stayed up until 3 a.m. writing about everything I was going through in my life at that point. I nearly cried writing because it was so depressing, but I just wrote and wrote. All I could think about was, I have to get good enough to make fifteen hundred dollars. I was excited the next day, I was telling everyone I'm going to be a comedian, no one believed me. I told my mom, she didn't believe me either. I was telling people in my neighborhood I was going to do comedy and how much they get paid. Almost everyone would tell me about this guy name bump city from our area who tried it at the improv and ran offstage. I had a friend say, "if you're serious then I know Larry Dog personally, I will call him now but you gotta tell me a joke" I said "you gotta be kidding right just call," he never called. I thought he was such a punk for not calling. I didn't realize how important it is not to put your name on everybody. I learned that lesson on my own along with everything else. I'm thinking man I'm just trying to do something with my life just help me. He never did.

It's crazy how things work sometimes. So, I'm sitting there and someone came up and said they heard I was thinking about doing comedy and I should call Trick Daddy because he owns the club. Trick Daddy is a famous rapper out of Miami who I just happen to come up with. If you knew his story you wouldn't be surprised why he's famous. He worked hard for years before he got his shot, but he was ready when it came. Long before he got his shot he acted like he had made it already. I called Trick Daddy and told him about me wanting to do comedy and he said, "call this number and tell him I said put you on stage tonight." I called, and it was Larry. He said "who's this and what you want" I told him what Trick said. He hung up on me. I called Trick back and he said, "call back and tell him if you don't get onstage he don't have a job." I called and told him what Trick said, he said "be there at 8." I got there, and I knew Larry still had no intentions on putting me onstage and I really didn't want to go on, but God had another plan. One of the comedians canceled last minute so one of the bouncers said, "man throw the little man up." Larry said, "what's your name?" I said, "SPUNKY!" He said, "you called me today?" "yes" "what's your name again, you got 5 minutes." That was the best-worst thing that has happened to me since my divorce. Not knocking my marriage at all but had I still been married no way I would be doing comedy. I thank God for what I went through because it gave me things to talk about. People love dramas, especially when it's not theirs. I was just able to make mine funny. I did great and my mom was even there to witness my first show though it was unplanned. Larry came over where we were and said, "this my boy right here, he's funny." You've got to love Larry Dog. I'm willing to bet he didn't know my name I think he was just happy I didn't bomb and made him look bad if I had to guess. I tell people it's like when a gambler wins big their very first time gambling they always think that they can win. That was me, I always think I'm going to do great. I found out that wasn't true. Thinking back, I can honestly say Trick Daddy helped me to start comedy. Had he not forced the issue I most likely wouldn't have either and probably would have given up thinking that it was a sign from God that I didn't get onstage. You know dreamers, we will find any reason not to. But you have to. A dream can't ever come true if you give up.

8. Work your work

Good things come to those who wait but only things left by those who hustle -Abraham Lincoln

When you think about comedy we mostly think about comedy clubs.   Mainly the ones that are in your city or closest. It's early 2010 and I had a good show under my belt in which now that I look back at it was horrible, but I was ready for the comedy clubs, so I thought. I called the club and they told me about this open mic they were having. I asked to be put on and then they told me I must have 10 people come to the show and say my name in order for me to perform. Houston, we have a big problem. Have my people come out on a Wednesday night just to see me do something nobody else we knew were doing? I think not. I just thought maybe it wasn't for me if I had to do all that and then I thought maybe just give it a shot and see what happens. What else am I going to do? I posted it all over Facebook went around the neighborhood giving out these free passes not really expecting people to come. I was just as some would say "shooting my shot." Well I'm not sure if they were there to see me succeed or get booed but about 65 people came that first night. I was so happy but so nervous at the same time. I'm talking about people I haven't seen in years showed up. I nearly raised the roof off of the club. At least I thought so. I was no more than the best of the worse that night. Now that I know comedy I'm convinced that my friends were just happy that I wasn't totally sorry, so they laughed. I thought that those fifteen hundred-dollar checks were coming soon. I was at my happiest at this point. I couldn't stop writing, couldn't stop talking about comedy. I'm amazed at the amount of people who thinks comedians just go onstage night in and night out be funny off the top of their head. I entered another contest at the comedy club and I told my dad I was going to be a comedian and I wanted him and his wife to come to my contest. My dad said, "I didn't raise no comedian." At first, I laughed because I thought he was joking. If you know my dad he's always in a joking mood for the most part. Then I realized he was actually serious this time. It kind of threw me off because I'm thinking he's going to be excited, but he wasn't. He showed up anyway and once again I rocked it. I think even he was surprised. I didn't win the contest because I didn't have a lot of people show up to cheer me on this time, but I was gaining more fans. It took about three contests to learn that it's not about who's the funniest or most talented that night, it's all about who can bring the most people have their friends spend money on food and drinks and cheer the loudest at the end of a night. Well at least where I'm from that's how it is. I never won a contest in South Florida. I actually cringe at the thought of doing them even today, but I take a different approach. I don't think about winning at all. My dad actually became one of my biggest supporters, he and my mom were fighting for first place. I tell other comics don't try to win contests, you will walk out frustrated night in and out. Instead get something out of it. Most club contest have pretty nice crowds and great lighting so it's a chance that if you have a good set it can be used to send to other bookers. Also network with the comics who you may not know. You will be surprised who you may meet. I also use it as an opportunity to try a few new jokes.

I've never understood how comedians go to any open mic and keep doing the same material and never at least try something new. Anything! I made up my mind that I would never do an open mic if I didn't have something new to say or worked on. It's useless doing proven material just to get laughs to stroke your own ego. I know these jokes are funny now let me build my set trying other jokes. I just wanted to be great. If I wasn't doing new material, then I was video recording my set, so I can send it to bookers. Still to this day that's my routine. Great stage, great lighting, good crowds, big laughs, yeah, I was using the time to help move me forward. I was expecting to lose all the contests and be number 17 out of 21 open mic comics but I didn't care, I was satisfied with what I had in my pocket, great footage. Many up and coming comedians really underestimate the real purpose of open mics. I get a little offended by comics that go onstage with nothing to say. They are on stage reaching for material in the room. I get a little upset. I think they do it probably because most open mics are mainly a room full of other comedians and maybe a few others who had absolutely nothing else to do that night, so they decided to hang with their comedian friend. I made it my duty to record every single open mic I did in my first few years. I didn't care about the laughs I just wanted to listen to my delivery and segways (I had no idea what that was at the time). I remember I would stay up until 3 am sometimes just dissecting each joke trying to see how can I add or take away from any particular joke to make it better. Sometimes I would just count how many times I cursed during a particular set. For some reason when you're a young comedian we think that curse words bring out the joke. Sometimes it may be necessary but it's always good to control your words and not really curse when it's unnecessary. The best way to control it is to write all your material with no swearing at all. It's easy to substitute words. Do not take open mics for granted though. It's practice for the real game. Lebron James and Tom Brady are probably the best at their sports right now today, but they still feel the need to practice every day. What's makes you different. Every comedian has done open mics at some point in their career. Unless you came up in the social media ranks but that's a different subject. No matter what road you decide to take you just can't stop.

9. Half Empty or Half Full

It doesn't matter if the glass is half empty or half full, drink up and STOP complaining

Most people let the word NO make or break their situation. I know I was almost one of those people. Now I try my best to let my No's be my motivation and so should you. I was one of those comedians that thought I had to get booked in the comedy clubs in order for it to validate me as a comic. If I can just get booked in the comedy clubs then I would be close to making it. Well still years later and I'm still waiting. Actually, by continuously being told no was the biggest blessing ever. I must admit it started to get a little frustrating just trying to get booked in my local comedy club. I mean I even questioned my talent at one point thinking I wasn't funny enough and that's why they wouldn't book me. Then I started going to a few shows and realized nah that's not it at all. I was told by other comics to just hang out and let them see you and maybe they will book you. I couldn't understand it, I'm saying so being funny is not good anymore I have to hang out on a Wednesday or Thursday night hoping they would be there just, so I can say hi look I'm here can you please book me. I was too stubborn to do that. Plus, I had work in the mornings. I even called to try to produce my own shows there and I would get the biggest run around known to man after seeing other young comics produce their own shows there and not ever being asked to do what I was asked. This went on for years until one day I made up my mind that I refuse to let a comedy club dictate how far I went in comedy. There is nothing stronger than a made-up mind. I really sat down and talked to God and realized that those few dollars they were paying people I could make that ten times over if I produced my own shows and book other comics that couldn't get booked in the comedy club. They were also talented but never received a chance to show it. Thing was that it wasn't ever about the money, I just wanted an opportunity. I only wanted a chance to show them that I could be good on their stage. I quickly realized I didn't fit in their circle. I didn't talk like them, I didn't write jokes like the others and I sure wasn't fake like a lot of them.   I didn't want anything to do with this city and the comedy scene because they really weren't giving most people that looked like me a solid chance. We were good to perform on "urban" night but anything passed that was not happening. I joke about it that they like African Americans, but they don't deal with the blacks. I want to say maybe I was a little bitter at the time. I came to realize that nobody owes you anything and people have a right to book and pay whoever they want. I then decided I would go to the city where folks that looked like me where given a real chance, Atlanta Georgia. I wasn't in Atlanta but three days then I knew when I left that that's where I needed to be. It was talent everywhere and I wanted to be in the midst of it all. I wanted to go and show Atlanta folks that I was just as talented as most of those comics there. I was really young in comedy and didn't understand that it was never a competition with those guys, I needed to be in competition with myself. I really wasn't ready to be onstage with so much talent that Atlanta had but my attitude told me otherwise. I was not me onstage and never even realized it. But then again who was I. I had watched so much comedy that I was practically someone else every month. Not telling their jokes but how I carried myself onstage. Earthquake, Kevin Hart, Mike Epps, hell even Deray Davis. I didn't even realize it until I started watching videos of myself. It was somewhat embarrassing in a way. A good friend of mine Sean Grant told me I probably won't find my comedic voice until about five years in, don't rush it. It's like a lot of new comics today, everyone wants to be great right now, so we often emulate our favorite comics.

In Atlanta though, majority of the seasoned comics had their own style. Some I had seen on T.V. and thought was talented. Every comic I would talk to would ask "what's going on in Miami" and I would always say "nothing at all." I just didn't want to talk about Miami. I actually thought why are you asking me about shows when you been on t.v., you've made it. I quickly learned that everything isn't what it seems in this business. Television doesn't mean you've made it.

Only to your friends and family it does. Television simply allows you to increase your price in most cases. Regardless my early years in comedy were probably my best days though, it's like when you hear people discuss a rapper and say that their earlier music was much better. When people are trying to make it there's a 24 hour a day 7 days a week fire that's inside of them, that was me. I was hungry, and I wasn't eating. I could go to Atlanta and move a little faster than I would in Miami, so Atlanta is the move. So, I thought.

A lot of times people make moves that are great for their careers but then sometimes not making moves is the best move. One thing I do is when I'm in the presence of veteran comics is listen. Of course, I treat everyone's information like a bag of weed. I take the seeds and sticks out the weed (useless information) and then all the good information I keep it, roll it up and smoke it. My friend comedian Double D said "hey man you can make it from anywhere. Think about it, it's maybe 5 or 6-real headliners in south Florida, it's 100 here in Atlanta. You will make more money here coming from out of town." He actually made a lot of sense to me. Thing was there weren't many stages to get on where I'm from and I just wanted to work. Then it hit me, why don't I just produce my own shows. Create my own stage, my own work. Thing is I knew absolutely nothing about running a comedy room. I just seen others put on shows but I had no real knowledge on what I was to do. I'm a firm believer that if someone doesn't want to give you work then you should create work yourself. You will be amazed when you are able to give people work how much work you can get. I started a small show with my best friend Derrick in an old Denny's. We rented chairs and tables and set it up how I saw some other rooms I had done. I think it sat maybe 50 people max. I think our total budget was $250 including the DJ and we split everything 50/50. I didn't have a lot of money at all. I think at the 1st show I didn't even have my half $125, so I borrowed about $75 with a promise I would give it back the next day. I was always told to have the show money when you arrive at the venue and never depend on the door. I hate when comedians/promoters depend on the door to pay entertainers. That's not business in my opinion. If someone makes an agreement with a comic for whatever the amount is then that amount at least should be in the bookers pocket when they arrive at the venue. What's really messed up about the comedy game is a booker will wait until after the comic has gone up and performed 20, 30, 45 minutes knowing they didn't have the money agreed upon before they went onstage. I don't understand how some people sleep after doing that to someone. Nobody wants to lose money but that's the risk we take when we decide to produce shows. If you can't stand to lose money, then don't take the risk. One important thing I've learned in this short time doing comedy is that your name is worth more than any dollar that you short someone. If you're a "janky promoter" trust me a lot of people know. If you run ghetto shows or great shows people know and if you're a joke thief people know. Whatever you put out their comedians will talk about. Your name goes a long way in this business whether it's good or bad. I told myself when I started producing my own shows my first order of business is to book people who have booked me in the past. It's only right to show love where love was shown. I also try to book every comic that I thought was funny around the city whether I liked them or not. I had vision of doing these big shows but for the moment I just wanted something small, something I could control because I didn't have a team of people to help run shows with me. I thought of a dollar amount that I know that I could pay each comic no matter if 2 people or 100 people showed up. I took pride on making sure comics I book walk away with every cent I agreed to. I remember once I booked a show for this promoter and he agreed to pay for the show. This is when I learned that all work is not good work. All I asked was for the comics to be paid before they touch the stage. Well before the show I go collect and he hands me about forty percent of what was agreed and said the crowd wasn't big, but he had more people coming and after the show he would give me the rest. At that moment something in my spirit said, "he's some bull" but my comics left their families to come rock with me so I said to the promoter, "man just look me in my eyes and promise all that money gone be here before the show is over." He shook his head to say yes so I went to start the show. Before I went onstage I went to the comics and I paid the feature in full and gave the closer what was left. Then I gave him my debit card and I said, "if you don't have your money by the time you get ready to leave then here's my pin number, go get the rest of your money and bring my card back." Seems crazy to some people but I knew my name is very important and I was gaining a little buzz in the south and I wasn't about to let some shady promoter ruin that. Of course, after the show the promoter didn't have all the money but what he did give me it covered the closer but I didn't make a penny but it didn't bother me at all. The lesson I learned about dealing with promoters was priceless though. There's always a lesson to be learned in business.

I know some of you are reading this thinks that's messed up that it happened but to be honest it happens more often than not. I've heard stories about janky promoters that made me leave and pray that nothing like those stories ever happened to me. I'm talking about bad situations. Actually, it's rather disturbing because I never hear about things happening like that in "non-urban" comedy shows. Not saying that it doesn't happen, but I've never heard not one story about it happening. Truthfully, it should never happen. It's a lot of lessons to be learned when you're in pursuit of your happiness. In my personal opinion the comedy world is very tainted these days. Most young comics want to be famous overnight, want to be funny right now and it doesn't happen like that for everyone. People want to skip the grind. People say It takes at least 10 years to be an overnight success. The grind is what makes you believe it or not. You can either be a true hustler and go get it, kiss booty and hope you're kissing the right one so they will help you out, or pray you somehow get tons of followers on social media to make it in entertainment. I think that's why most veteran comedians respect me as a comic. Veteran comedians see me grinding like they had to in order to make it. They see me city to city, state to state on buses, airplanes, trains just like they had too. We are in an internet age where a person can sit in front of a video recorder and shoot some videos, have some great editing and a few sound effects and gain a big enough following on social media to get booked to come host events without ever having to leaving their city. I can see how that can be frustrating to someone who's been really grinding for years and years and all of a sudden, you're opening up for an "internet sensation." Do not get me wrong I have absolutely nothing against internet sensations because your blessing is your blessing, but I can see why real veteran comics can feel some type of way about the way they are getting it. I've even seen social media comedians diss veteran comics and have 2200 comments of their followers rooting them on. This happens when you didn't work hard for your success and don't fully understand what some comics went through to get to where they are. Once you realize only real stuff last and everything else is here today and gone tomorrow it'll be less frustrating. No matter what stick to doing you. It's too hard trying to be like someone else. I try not to even pay attention to people that are big on the internet because unless they find some other gimmick most don't be around too long. It's getting so bad now because everyone is putting on a wig and a dress and acting like ghetto women to gain followers. I mean really, it's cool (it's really not) but years from now after you've gotten popular doing it and you're in your mid- thirties or early forties, is that all you want to be known for. It's gotten so popular and easy to do that white folks are jumping on board. I'd rather be warm all year than to be fire hot in the summer but the rest of the year I'm cold as ice. To each his own though. Consistency and discipline is important while you're grinding. No matter what don't give up. You can't just be casual when pursuing your purpose because by being casual you will end up a casualty.

10. Plan your pursuit

Dreams without goals remains just dreams.

When you are in pursuit you should do it aggressively. Some people write down their goals for the year around New Year's Day and rarely look at it again. I write mine down and read it daily. You gotta utilize the law of attraction. The universe wants you to win you just gotta keep reminding it about your willingness to win. You should work towards your purpose at some point every day if possible. So, what you have a job that takes up a lot of your time. That should be more of an incentive for you to get off your butt and start planning your escape route. If you don't have time, then create time. If I told you, you have 30 days to lose 10 pounds and you would be rewarded one million dollars if you accomplished it you would find a way to lose 10 pounds. Probably so. Same schedule, same job, same bills. That tells me that your dreams are not that important to you just yet. Create time for your dreams. I walked off my job just 3 years into doing comedy. I had $38 dollars in the bank and my oldest son living with me at the time. It didn't make sense to anyone why I would make such a crazy decision, but it made perfectly good sense to me. I wasn't trying to make sense. I just knew I was tired of waking up going to a job and helping some company build their dream while I had dreams of my own. I believe since we only have one life to live I was determined to be happy and I wasn't. How many times have you logged on to social networks at 9 am and someone is saying "hurry up 5 o'clock." I say you just clocked in. That's no way to live life. I understand that we have bills that needs to be paid so I'm by no means telling anyone to walk off their job. But what you can do is find your goals, write them down and be specific. Most people will tell you their goals are things like to have money, or be in good health or happiness. These are not goals, these are just general things desired by everyone. Take your time and think about what you really want out of this life and be specific. Make goals for 5 years, 1 year, 6 months, month to month, and even daily goals. Before I go to sleep I write down everything I want to accomplish for the next day. I get a lot more done planning out my day. It also helps when I get off track I always go back to what was my plans for the day. Get a deadline date that you want certain something you're working towards done, this will help you focus more on your target. Even if it doesn't meet the target goal date, you will be much closer than you would've been had you not even started. You're going to find yourself coming in from work and working a little towards your goals and before you know it all your free time will consist of working on your work. Start small, people often forget that baby steps are still steps. You don't have to be great to start but you have to start to be great. We live in this microwave society where we want everything fast, but it doesn't always happen that way. It may take you twice as long and twice the money but stay focused and keep going. The hardest thing to do when you're up and coming is to not quit. I spent a lot of days frustrated with the process of becoming a comedian. I had seen guys that I had done shows with the night before on television the next night. I would always ask "when will my time come." It felt like God had said man it's been your time. Thing is I didn't want it bad enough I just kind of wanted it. I had to sit back and ask myself was I really working my absolute hardest and I was not. It's important that you be completely honest with yourself and your hustle. I had been looking at a lot of comedy on television and I thought to myself that I know I'm funny, but I was missing something before I get my shot at television. It took me almost a year to realize things truly happen for specific reasons and there is nothing worse than getting your big opportunity and not being ready for it. I thank God that I wasn't thrown on any major stages when I thought I should have because now that I look back I wasn't ready. It's necessary to go through the process in order to appreciate where you came from. When chasing a dream, it's really scary not knowing where the road ends but I think that's the greatest part of the journey, not knowing. Truth be told many of us would not ever pursue our dreams if we could actually see what it will take to make it. The blood, the sweat, the real tears, the empty bank accounts, family sacrifices, and for some the loneliness. I'm not sure I would have continued pursuing comedy had I knew exactly what it would take, I will be honest.

I never ever thought I would sleep in airports, bus stations, or sometimes total strangers' houses just to save a dollar for the next trip. Very hungry and uncomfortable a lot. I guess those days of being homeless was somehow preparing me to learn how to be comfortable in uncomfortable situations. I was taking 19-hour bus trips for just a few hundred dollars. Even today doing something like that doesn't make sense to the average person. I'm not average! You can't be average. I never ever take a gig without a calculated step in helping me in my career. That's why you can't tell people things about your career moves sometimes because people will talk you right out of the move. Every show I've been on I made sure I got something out of it. Even if I didn't do so well. I say that because I don't bomb, I may not do as well as I know I could, but I always learn something so that's not a bomb. Instead it's a lesson. How can you bomb attempting to do something most people you know won't dare to do ever? You at least took a leap of faith to do something out of the norm. You just aren't that good at your craft yet, keep trying. Think about it, in football, if you'd gotten beat for the game winning touchdown because you were out of position doesn't make you a loser. You and your team may have lost that particular game but what you learn in the process is what's important. That feeling you had by getting beat for the game winner you probably don't ever want again but how are you going to prevent it. You watch film on the play. Look at your technique and positioning on the play to make sure you get rid of bad habits so that it won't happen again. Same thing goes for bombing. That feeling you have after you put the mic back on the stand and walk off stage and no one clapped, or they were clapping because you finally got off stage is not a great feeling at all but how do you make sure it doesn't happen again. I've learned more from my not so good performances than I've ever did from my great ones. We don't get overall better by continuously working on your strengths, you do so by working on the weaknesses. No matter how long you are on a grind you never stop learning. The problem with pursuing a purpose, most people want the shine but not the grind. It took 20 years to be 20 years old right? But the lessons you learned and things you went through is what made you who you were.

11. Don't Expect Love from Your Hometown

People you know won't support you until you no longer need their support

The biggest mistake I made was thinking once I get a little name for myself on comedy that my friends from Miami would be happy for me and support my movement. I was so wrong. It almost sent me in a little depressed state seeing how many people I knew that wouldn't support anything I was doing. Most entertainers who made it to be really successful out of the city moved away then became successful. Someone told me Jesus never got any love in his city either, he left and received more love and that changed things for me. I left. Then I found out most young comics across the nation really weren't getting good support at home, but I didn't care I wanted Miami to support me. I was okay when I found out that majority of your support will come from people who were not a family member or were not a friend or didn't grow up with you. Not that I don't appreciate the support I just couldn't understand. No matter how successful you are you are still "just you." to them. As successful as Oprah and Kevin Hart is to people they grew up with they are just Oprah and Kev. Don't let it bother you. Most real supporters will be people that you will meet while doing comedy. People that know nothing about you. It's not that your friends/family don't want to support your dream, they just don't like where they will be sitting when your dream actually comes true. It made sense. No matter how high you climb the ladder to success you're always the person that was in class with me. Kevin Hart as big as he is, is still Kev that use to stock shoes with me. He's not the Kev that worked his butt off to achieve massive success. And for some strange reason whenever you do get to that great level of success everyone knew you would make it. Don't get bothered just keep moving. When you start making a name for yourself in your city you will know because you will start getting fake conversations and fake support. Many conversations will consist of people asking you when the next show is as if they were going to show up. They will tell you to let them know so they can come but most people won't. People will have a full conversation with you about everything, every city, and every celebrity you posted on your social media but will never show up to a show or even like the picture unless it's their favorite celebrity in which they aren't liking the pic for you they are liking the celebrity. Those are the people who are waiting for you to blow up, so they can tell others that they know you. Don't be upset with them but understand who they are. I have some people that have never seen me perform unless they were there to support someone else. I remember I opened up for Mike Epps at this venue not too far from my neighborhood. At this point I had been producing my own shows in the same area for about two years at this point and could barely get people to come out. The night of the Mike Epps show the building was standing room only. I mean people I hadn't seen in years. People I thought moved away from Miami it was crazy. Tickets were $45 and $55 at the door and they paid it. I learned a lesson that night that people are going to spend their money and support what they want. You can't be mad at that. I hear comics talk about the price of other more successful comedian tickets are and how their friends pay all that money to see them when they only charge $10 to come to their show. I always say hey man they just don't support you like that. If they are not supporting, then they are not important. We worry so much about who's not supporting that we forget to be thankful for those who do. Concentrate on those who want to support you and those that don't simply don't exist in my world. I have this thing that irritates me, and it's called fake support. Those people that will support you if it's at a discount or free. I had a comedy friend name Pookie, really talented comedian that has been doing comedy for a while but never really had any guidance when it came to his career. Really funny and talented writer but He love comedy so much that he would give people crazy discount prices for shows just to get onstage. He would call me, and we must have had the same conversations over and over about getting on the road, how to sell yourself, pricing and running shows. He's a microphone fiend which is great, but his business side was close to being awful. I had to tell him that he has to learn how to say no. He wasn't calling people trying to get on shows they were calling him which means he had a little leverage. You can't make demands until you're in demand. Know what you are worth and the value the show brings to your career. What are you trying to gain from this show besides money. Especially when people call you to perform. People will call you and ask you to come perform an hour for a price that that barely covers your gas and beer money. No matter how successful you are people don't see being a comedian as a real job. We used to talk about when he produces his own shows don't reduce your tickets just, so people will show up. If the room only seat 50 people and you have 3 comics to pay plus your DJ then why charge only $5 entry fee. You're doing a show just to say you did one. At the end of the night everyone is going to go home happy and you will have to borrow money for gas tomorrow. Your time and effort is money. You still have bills also. I would rather be at a show with 10 people that paid their money that want to really be there than 50 people that I had to give a discount or free tickets, so they would show up. I'm a firm believer of I don't care how many people showed up as long as you make sure they enjoy themselves. I'm not saying don't ever show love to people but if you show love and give discounts or free tickets give them to people who's been supporting you. You have people that will use you to try to seem like someone. They have family/friends in town and all of a sudden, they want to come to the show but with a hook up. Other people will bring you up in conversation and all of a sudden y'all are so cool. These same people won't share a flyer on social media, won't share a video on social media, won't even like a post that they may agree with just because it's you. Don't be bothered by any of this. It's amazing how people make social media likes so important when it's not. God don't need who's not supporting you or what you don't have he simply will use what you do have to make you great, but you can't allow what you don't have to overshadow what you do have. Start where you are with what you have because what you have is enough.

12. Everyone is Not Going to Like You

Stop looking for love in all the wrong places

One big mistake up and coming comedians make is that we think that everyone will like you. Why not we are in the funny business right. Well if you are in this to be like then go ahead and quit now. Free up the prayer line for someone else. To be honest you shouldn't even be here to be liked you should be here to try to create a life for yourself doing something you love to do. Understand when you start climbing the ladder to success there will be comedians who you had done shows with, shared stories with and sometimes even paid money for shows will be the first to throw dirt on your name. This is a good thing, you're on the right track but don't try to figure out why they are attacking you just keep focused and keep going. The worst mistake you can make is to think everyone will do things like you may do them. It happened to me, but I always tell everyone that I'm a grown man first before I was ever a comedian so the way I will deal with betrayal outside of comedy I dealt with it during comedy, I didn't. I always said why argue back and forth with people? When you are done arguing they are still going to be the same person, so you are wasting your time. Just cut them off immediately. Understand people don't become certain ways after they become an entertainer they have been like that their entire life. Entertainment just brought it to light.

If you know me, talked to me or ever worked with me you know I really believe in helping others as much as I can. I think service in anything is important. I believe my blessings comes from service and helping others. But I found out that everyone is not worthy of even being helped. Some people are bottom feeders. They stay close enough to you just in case you do something big in the industry, so they can make that "put ya boy on" call to you. It's crazy how so many people can tell you how to be successful when they are not themselves. They are not practicing what they preach. Here's my crazy story.

So, when I started comedy in Miami there were a few comics that had been doing things around the city. Most had been had all doing comedy around 9 years at this time. They weren't popular anywhere outside the city, but they were known somewhat in the city. One comic even started the same exact day I did. We were close for the most part. Mainly because we were all black. We had written together, we did skits together, we were practically one in the same. So, we all would hit the scene night in and night out trying out new jokes and being really competitive about who will have the best set for the night. Times were good. The only bad thing about me going out four or five days a week doing comedy is that my license was suspended for 5 years from the two refusals to take the DUI test in 2009 and again in 2011. So, I was basically throwing rocks at the jailhouse (risking my freedom) several times a week just to tell jokes. I was sort of glad when my aunt Tara sold the car she had given me to get to shows and to help me get back on my feet. That kept me from driving late at night. I wasn't going to stop driving to shows on my own. I would still catch buses and trains or bum rides to get to and from shows though. So, a year and a half in comedy and my friend decided to stop comedy and become a rapper. It was cool because he was pretty good at it. I supported him. I played the CDs, I told others about him also. Shortly after he fell off the comedy scene completely and myself and others kept doing comedy in the city. I started producing my own comedy shows in Miami and I booked the other comics that the comedy club wouldn't book on everything that I produced. Everything! Over the years I started working with other promoters to host other shows in other cities. Tallahassee, FL, Panama City, FL, Kissimmee, FL, Georgia and Miami so I was really busy. I was barely even in Miami anymore and things were good. One day I received a call from a fellow comedian telling me that the guys were calling him asking him why I wasn't booking them for out of town shows. I was lost. I actually tried to book two of them. It was going to be a Miami takeover show in Tallahassee. Long story, but within two days of the show after being promoted all month both canceled leaving me to book an entire show last minute. I didn't mind because I knew a lot of comics, but the promoter told me not to book anyone else from Miami ever again. I tried to help but this is the thanks I received. I understand things happen, but they had no real reason why they couldn't come. I explained to one that he should book his bus ticket now, so it would be really low, but he didn't and by the time he tried to it was somewhat expensive and he cancelled the show saying the money wouldn't be worth it after purchasing his bus ticket. The other waited until 2 days before the show to try to get a flight in which he knew he wouldn't be able too. They never really left the city before then, so I guess fear sat in, but I didn't care I learned my lesson. This went on for years. Crazy part is no one ever asked me why I wouldn't book them out of town. I only deal with people who are really serious about what we are doing. I only booked one comic from Miami on an out of town show in the next three years after that and he was my cousin Chicken George. Years went on all of a sudden, I get a call.

> Comic: Aye bro why are they attacking you like that what did you do?
>
> Me: What are you talking about?
>
> Comic: On ya boy page they are saying you took their jokes.
>
> Me: Huh? You stupid. When this happened?
>
> Comic: Like a week ago. Go on his page. They are calling me talking about you, but I keep telling them to call you. Go look if you want.

At this point I'm thinking so this guy crawled from up under a rock to start comedy again because rap didn't work and now he trying to throw rocks at the sun but can't look at it in the face. Not that I was famous by any stretch of imagination, but I was way more popular than any young comic in the city. I'm not that same fellow he knew. I go to his page. Wait, he deleted me. So, you delete me then talk lies about me. At Least if you're going to talk about someone tag the person so they will know. I didn't even know he had beef with me about anything. I didn't think that because I had just had him on my show in Panama City less than a month ago. I sat down with him at the hotel and I explained to him what I knew about comedy while I smoked a cigar. His post said something in the likes of he just got a call from someone about his joke being told in a city he's never been in. Someone asked who was telling his jokes and he said my name. I was floored. I laughed. I laughed even harder at the other comics who were commenting on the post like I had stolen their jokes also. One thing I do not like is when someone has a problem on social media all the other yes men come from nowhere and say what they been wanting to say but never had the courage to speak up. I was mad, not at the fact that he was trying start a beef he was clearly not ready for but because they all had my phone number and could've easily called me and said whatever they had to say. We are men, right? You all are grown, and some have been doing comedy for years and barely leave the city right? I don't play internet games and they know that, so I picked up the phone myself. I call one of the other comics first and asked what joke are you talking about and be specific. He says, "my Beyoncé joke." I said, "post it on my page and ask anyone have they ever heard me say anything close to any Beyoncé joke." I asked who told you I stole your joke, call them. He wouldn't, and I said man you are lying, and you know it. Are you upset because I'm progressing past you in comedy or is it because I won't book you out of town? Thing is I was never in any competition with any of them in my head but in theirs I guess I were. The funny part is that he spent 20 minutes telling me what he has and sending me pictures of his house and car but none of it came from doing comedy, so the conversation didn't make sense. I was happy that he was doing good in life truly. I want people I'm cool with to win. I didn't know he secretly thought I was taking his jokes. I thickened the plot just a little when a joke he had been telling for some time I posted the actual video of the other person's joke word for word on the post and asked anyone have they ever heard that joke in Miami. Problem was his joke was nowhere online so how could someone who's never met you steal from you. Within 4 minutes the video disappeared. I had been knowing about the jokes for a while, but I don't care I just do me. I'm not the comedy police. What I won't let you do is try to assassinate my character because you are bored. I got back online and practically begged the other two to just call me. By this time another comic had tagged maybe 50 comics trying to make me look bad. He was unaware of the pettiness I'm capable of. They will post but won't call so I called him. He won't answer. 9 calls and you won't answer. Cool, so I'm going to come to your world.   I said" hey man aren't you the same comic who told me and several other young comics not to ever write jokes, you just take people jokes and remix them?" I couldn't understand why he would dare say anything. I felt like Tupac in the song Hit Em UP. I'm like "YOU...YOU!" I said, "as a matter of fact you tagged the big comedians in Miami but aren't they the same guys you called me and said you tired of them stealing your material and I laughed and said get the heck out of here with that?" YOU! So, everyone is stealing your material that's not even yours? I hated going there because I'm so peaceful, but this was like fighting my little brothers. I felt a little hurt because again they have my phone number. Let's deal with my young homie now. He posts a video of the joke I supposedly stole from him. First of all, what he didn't tell the internet was that it was my punchline. Any comic will tell you that we are never upset about the setup of a joke we are mad at punchlines that gets taken. As a matter of fact, I don't even do the joke the same anymore because his part was weak. Second of all anyone can film a joke, put it online and say it's theirs, it was weak. So, me being sarcastic because he had called me out my name and now I was just going to beat his face up I posted saying yeah, I took your joke please do something about it. This guy screenshot what I said and made it seem like I actually admitted something I didn't do. Then I started getting phone calls. Real friends telling me to not entertain those people concentrate on your brand. You've come too far to even look back. They were absolutely correct. I lost myself for a minute but I'm back. I went and deleted every comment I ever wrote and let them say what they wanted to say about me. I didn't care. They were feeling like I owed them something because I knew them, but I didn't. I had to be real with myself. I told myself Spunky when you were sleeping in bus stations, in airports, on females couches, taking 12 hours bus rides, not seeing your children for a month, not seeing your lady friend for weeks, sometimes starving, walking in the rain and sometimes the snow just chasing a dream they were home playing with their children going on dates, being at all the parties and sleeping next to their girlfriend every night and now that you are doing something they want in, the devil is a liar. Nope, I'd rather book comics that may not be as funny but is out here trying to get better. Those few days changed my thought process about friends and the people you have around you. It's a shame when females began to be truer than the men. Times have changed. I knew I wasn't immune to anything that happen in this industry but never in 100 years would I thought it would come from people who I broke bread with. Who I wrote jokes with. Who I shared a drink with. No matter what they were trying to do it went nowhere but God taught me something. I learned the lesson and kept it moving.

13. *Be Willing to Sacrifice*

Be willing to sacrifice a good time for every dime or you want to make

I often get asked how do I get so much work doing comedy in such a little amount of time that I've been doing it with no manager or anything. I first correct them and tell them that God is my manager and then I tell them that if they are not prepared to do what I'm willing to do to make it then we shouldn't be having this conversation. I can give 100 people my exact blueprint on how I get work and why I do it that way and do it with confidence because I know 98 of the won't do it. Reason being because it's not easy and it's often frustrating. People see comedians or entertainers in general when they are "moving" and they want that but very few people knows exactly what it takes. If you are truly serious about making it then realize unless your finances is in order then don't even think about going full time. Have yourself at least three months of mostly paid shows booked before you even consider going full time. If you have a family make sure they are okay with your decision and is fully aware of what it will take before you pursue it because the amount of time it's going to take to really get your name out there some would call ridiculous. If you are single it may be best to remain that way until you get a little established. Unless you get that women on your team that fully understand what it will take to pursue your purpose. I can't tell you how many times I've listened to women say that they can handle my lifestyle until they are knee deep in it. It takes a really strong person to deal with an entertainer. It's a lot of women around, a lot of week's when we wouldn't see each other, the money isn't always that great. It's very frustrating at times. Also, be prepared to be lonely. I've traveled so much all these years that I'm most comfortable only when I'm alone. Stay focused on yourself always. Laser focused! People often get thrown off by what others think of them or what others have to say about them and their craft. One simple thing I learned in life is that people are going to talk about you regardless of whether you are doing good or bad. They great part is you can use that as a motivational tool. Use it to turn you on. Dogs don't bark at parked cars, only cars that's moving somewhere. People don't talk about people who aren't doing anything. One thing young comics make the mistake of wanting to just travel all over. I told myself I'm going to be the best in my area then I'm going to start branching out to the cities and states closest to me. Places you can go and turn around and come right back home. Trust me if you're making enough noise in your city people will hear about it. Comedians talk like high school best friends. Another mistake is young comics make is they're always screaming show me the money. Yeah, it's great to get paid but that can't be your only motivation. If it is then stop reading now and give this book to someone else. You do this because you love it. And because you love it you are trying to be the best at it and if you're not trying to be the best at it why are you doing it. When you become the best version of yourself the money will come but don't just focus on the money. I've spoken with numerous comedians that won't leave their city because they won't make a lot of money on a particular show. I'm not mad at them at all but that is the end of our conversation always. I revisit the cities and they are still there trying to score the big payday. No one will ever know who you are unless to go show them who you are. Make plans to go to different cities whenever you can afford too. Save up, go to some cities that have a few rooms or shows in a particular week. Reach out to whoever books the shows and ask for a guest spot. Most likely they will allow you too because they don't have to pay you to entertain their audience. They more than likely will give you only five minutes but that's all you need. Do not take this opportunity for granted. I always tell any comedian when you leave your city MAKE SURE YOU ARE FUNNY AND PROFESSIONAL. A lot of times when you go do good on your guest spots the booker actually sees you live and considers booking you for a paid spot. Understand you are going to have some comics tell you they wouldn't do it because it's not worth it. Those comedians you stay away from. Surround yourself with likeminded people, with people are understand that it's truly a hustle and grind.

The thing I sacrificed the most is the time

with my children. It's some people out there aren't willing to even consider that, but I was in a position that I could stay home and barely survive and barely help them anyway or I could sacrifice time with them while they were still young to be able to live a good life when they are older. It was basically a no brainer for me. I wasn't doing anything in Miami anyway. I could barely afford McDonalds when they asked. I didn't have transportation to even go see them most of the time. I wasn't able to send a few dollars for child support. Even when I could see them I had no place to stay or for them to stay so I would have to ask family can they stay there just to spend a day or two with them on weekends. I was no good to myself let alone my children. I'm at a point to where I'm gone so much that I miss so many accomplishments that they have, and they call just wanting to spend time for the weekend but I'm in another state so I can't. It saddens me when that happens. I even get online sometimes and see others with their child at school or at a party and it saddens me, but I had to stay focused. I knew if I go back just for that purpose I wouldn't help the situation. I had no other income yet that will allow me to take time off to chill. One thing I will do is call or text almost every single day. I can't see them that often, but I made sure we communicated. Sometimes your kids just want to hear from you. I did what I was able too and when I did get free time I try to pick them up even if it was for a few hours. I had refused to not have a relationship with my children no matter the circumstances. I can say I sacrificed having money also, but I was only making $7.35 a hour and with child support getting taken out of that I figured if I work 8 hours a day towards perfecting my comedy craft and hustle as hard as I can I can make the money I'm making at that job and do what I love to do and see the world. That's it. Sudden decision I made because I was unhappy where I was in life. Had I known how hard it would be to make money I'm not sure I would've quit my job. I had to do something though. I'm a firm believer and I will say it 100 times. When someone doesn't want to give you work then just create your own work. Create your own shows. Nobody ever told me that I just figured that out on my own somehow. You don't even have to have a big budget to do so. You will be surprised about the caliber of comedians I've had on my shows for only $100. One thing about comics we are always trying to stay onstage. Great thing about Miami was a lot of people vacationed there so when they knew they were coming on vacation they would call to see of they can make a few dollars while in the city. It happens week in and week out across the country. A comic maybe coming to your city to do a weekend at the local comedy club and have to fly in early. If you have a Thursday night comedy show you may get lucky and have them bless your stage for whatever you room pays. If you can't afford to go to different cities, then bring comedians from different cities to you. It's great for networking and you always have a platform to work your jokes and build a following in your city. Remember to always run good quality shows through. The type of show you run is the type people will label you as. It can be weekly, bi-weekly monthly or every other month whatever you feel you can handle. It may be slow at first, but you can't give up on it. I had a show in Panama City for 10 straight months and the promoter and I lost money. I was catching two buses there each month to lose money, but we didn't give up. We moved our venue and the very next month the show were sold out. That's when I found out location of an event is important also. Still today which is over two years later we are still producing good shows with good audiences.

Don't give up when the sky isn't blue. It's a building process but you've got to be patient and willing to work hard to build it.

14. The Not So Glory Road

Cool head warm feet.
Translation: always stay calm and
always keep it moving

In order for you to really do what you need to do to be successful you MUST get comfortable with being uncomfortable. I will say this over and over.   Often things go wrong on the road. Shows get canceled, you don't get paid all the money agreed to, flights delayed, buses break down. As a matter of fact right now as I'm writing I'm on a Megabus headed home from Virginia in which I left Tuesday at 4:30 pm and was supposed to reach Atlanta at 7:30 am to catch a flight to Miami at 12:40 pm. Instead, my bus broke down in North Carolina at 1:00 am and didn't get fixed until 2:00 pm. Long story short, I missed my flight so instead I had to take another 12-hour bus ride to get home. Most people would be discouraged by all that happening, but I always tell myself to control what you can control and don't let life's setbacks get you upset. I just kept telling myself that God is keeping me from something, so I smiled and gladly took the ride. That's was just this week's episode. It's a plethora of stories similar to that I can tell you about.

Another lesson I've learned is not to put too much faith in people. That way I'm never disappointed. I met this woman at a show in Atlanta and we kept in touch off and on for a while. I knew I would be going through Atlanta a lot so maybe I could stay with her if we are cool enough and save money on hotels. Before you think that's crazy staying with someone I really didn't know understand that it happens on the grind way more than most people know about. Basically, I was in a Airbnb before Airbnb. When you take a leap of faith to pursue your dreams it becomes a fight for survival and a lot of that survival depends on people you meet in these different cities. You may need a ride to or from the airport or shows. You may need somewhere to crash for a few hours before you next bus or flight. Something as simple as a meal or a familiar face is important. Well she agreed to let me crash at her house for the weekend since her kids were going to be gone. We spoke the entire week prior to me coming because I didn't want any misunderstanding when I got there. It wasn't about sex for me at all, it was about shelter and the fact that I would save almost two hundred dollars. We spoke on the Megabus ride up there and things were cool. As soon as I got to Atlanta it was cold and drizzling. I stepped of the bus and she no longer would answer the phone calls or text messages. It was unbelievable. I wasn't even upset. I wasn't disappointed with her, I was upset with myself for trusting the situation. She had that right to change her mind at any point. She was doing me a favor but at least tell me is what I was stressing. I didn't know what to do so I walked about three miles in the cold and rain to the greyhound station so at least I could be indoors until I figured something out. I went to sleep for a few hours at the station cold and wet then decided to call Sweet baby Kita, a comedy friend of mine. I called her because I learned that with most comics they will tell you to call them when you get in town and when you get in town no one is available or won't answer the call, but she always came through. She came to pick me up and we spoke about what had happened and if you know her she made jokes about that for the entire weekend, but she saved my weekend. One thing about her is when she's your friend then you can't do no wrong except in her eyes. She and people like her are great people to know. That taught me to not take anyone's word for anything and always be prepared because often things will often go not as planned. No matter what keep going.

I did a show in Tallahassee once at a venue that sat about 5,500 people. I was supposed to host the show but days before I chose to just do my 20 minutes and sit down. I asked my buddy to host it. He had been on the road hosting shows for this big headliner for a few years now. There had also been two more comics that had been in the business 20 plus years. Show started late because the balance of our pay wasn't in the building. That's when I really seen that no matter how much you love to do something that when it's your livelihood it's still about business. I had been hosting a show in the city for years now, so I knew people that were there so I'm getting so many call and texts about when the show would start. I didn't have answers. I was just enjoying my own dressing room watching football until someone gave me the word. It's an hour past when the show was supposed to start, and no one is there except me the host and another opener. The headliner wouldn't even leave the hotel until his money was paid. All I'm seeing is people rushing from one room to the next back to the other room. Finally, the show started. Everyone did an awesome job. I stood around all the veteran comics who weren't on stage and just listened to stories about comedy. Then the headliner goes onstage, he put on a show like I've never seen. Nonstop funny. I walk to my dressing room to grab my DVD's to go sell after the show and I can hear the headliner say, "well I'm about to get out of here." When he said that two men who were in the back with me walked out the back door as if they were in a hurry. I didn't think nothing of it, but they were two of the men going from room to room earlier. I go sell all my DVD's and come back and everyone is looking worried.

I'm happy because I made a little money though. I asked, "hey what's wrong?" My partner/promoter who helped put the show together said, "we can't find the other promoters." I knew those words weren't good. They were gone. I found out that the two guys that walked out the back door were the promoters of the shows and had ran off with the balance of all of our money. The sum of close to 25 thousand dollars combined. My promoter who help set the show up said, "man let's go to their hotel room right now." Me being from Miami I knew they were not there. I said, "fam they are headed back to where they came from." It was bad. I needed my money, but I was getting paid the least, so I didn't take it as hard as some of the bigger comedians. I took my lost under the chin. The other comics didn't take it so well. One comics brother even threatened shooting my promoter if he didn't find the other promoters with the money. They took a huge lost. Myself and my promoter learned very good lessons night. I learned to always get a deposit from people if it's over a certain amount of money and always asked to be paid before the show. MY promoter learned all money and propositions are not good one's especially when large amounts of money is involved. I know he took it very hard that we didn't get our money because he is a man of integrity. He could care less about his money he just wanted ours. It left a very bad taste in everyone's mouth but through it all we never stopped.

15. You Don't Promote You!

How will people know who you are if you don't tell them

Before I go any further I must say if you are not promoting yourself every single day in some way then I'm not sure what you are doing in entertainment. Especially if you're up and coming. I always hear entertainer's say they don't like social media and don't want to be on it. To that I say that is insane. Social media has made more people famous and financially stable in the last few years than anything else. You may not like it but it's the way of the world right now. How would anybody know who you are or what track you're on in your career if you don't show them. A flyer here, a picture there. Something to say I'm still out here. You would be amazed by how many people you alone help to not give up just by them seeing your progress. People are always looking for a reason to not give up and sometimes it's other people's grind that helps them to not give up. Some say move in silence. That's cool also but if you don't have a popular name and or a good following how would you ever get one if you don't promote you, if you're in silence. You ever heard the term out of sight out of mind. If people don't see you it doesn't mean that you aren't working but if I don't know you are then how support, it or book you. I can't tell you how many times I've seen comics post stuff and in the comment section someone's saying hey I want to book you for a show hit me up please. It's happened to me on several occasions. I've also seen a flyer put out with a comic that's been doing it for a while and someone comments, "they still do comedy." People don't know unless you let them know. People don't know you're having financial issues or marital problems until you post it and let the world know. Same concept here. We have Facebook, Twitter, Instagram, Snapchat and a few other social media apps that will allow you to reach the masses in just a few minutes. Take advantage of it. Get creative. Think, why are you following the people you are following? What makes you go check out their page every now and then? No matter how you look at it almost everyone is using social media to build their brand or stay afloat. You are a comedian/entertainer. Promoters don't know but a small percentage of us that's out here but what they do know is that they can find a funny comic in almost every city they reach. What they won't find is an entertainer that can fill up a venue on their name alone in every city the reach. If you do not already have an established name I have some great news. Social media allows you that opportunity daily. Promote you and your brand as much as you can. People won't ever share or like or even comment but they see. From the highest up to the lowest of the lows. But give them something to pay attention too not just look at. Every time I see an actor, a television host, a talk show host I smile and think man they did all that just doing exactly what I'm doing. What a life. You can't get there by being lazy, by watching everything someone else is doing and not getting up to get your own hustle on. By nor willing to sacrifice. In comedy you are either in the way or on your way. If you're in the way, move out the way and if you feel you're on the way go all gas with no brakes. Do not stop.

16. Deal with Bookers the Right Way

Some people charge a fee, some of us charge what we are worth.

When you've been doing it for a while and you start dealing with different bookers you start to get a feel how to deal with your bookings. I was never taught how to price myself when it came to shows so I would always start high and make them work me low. Sometimes I would get lucky and they go for the high price and I would be thinking to myself for real. I look at it like working a 9 to 5. Someone making 10 dollars an hour and works 8 hours then they are paid $80. The difference is I work minutes. If someone wants me to do a 10, 15, 30-minute set then I ask myself what am I worth per minute. Ten, fifteen, twenty dollars per minute according to size of the venue and a few other things. Now I'm at the point that I just ask what their budget for the show.

Sometimes we can underprice ourselves. The promoter was willing to pay one thousand but you only said three hundred so that was a deal to them. No promoter is going to say man I will give you $700 instead. If they give you a price that you don't like, then its other ways to negotiate more money. You may get a hotel discount or know someone in the city that you can crash with so ask for that money they were going to pay for your hotel with. Always look and see what it will cost you to travel before making deals. Nothing is worse that telling someone you will perform for $400 and you travel cost is $378 round trip. I've learned to always ask for a deposit to hold their date. It's an awful feeling to pass up on several shows keeping your word on a date with no deposit then the show is canceled. I tell comics all the time to make people pay to cancel. I don't hold any dates until I receive my deposit period. If the amount is not a big dollar amount I may just choose to get all the money when I get there but I will then ask out of respect can I just get paid before I perform. People with good intentions don't have a problem with that. If you are getting the run around about that then you should lift up your spidey senses. Some bookers have trust issues about paying people before shows but look at it this way. If a comic shows up and you pay them then they leave, then it's something wrong with that comic in life not just comedy. If a booker has all the intentions on paying their talent, then why not pay before they go onstage. I feel it's just good business. I've been at shows with little or no money and wanted a drink or food and couldn't get it because the promoter wanted to pay after the show. Some promoters will want to pay you after the show and then clean up the entire building and talk to everyone in the building before paying you. It's horrible. Thing is what young comics don't clearly don't understand is that we run this business not the promoters. We often give way too much power to the promoters. Yes, they are paying for the show but there is no show without us. Promoters can sometimes turn comics against one another trying to save money for themselves. Do not ever undercut or talk bad about another comic to a promoter. When the promoter stops doing shows you will still have to deal with that comic. When it's time to hit the road, the promoter is not jumping in the car with you all. It's not good to make many enemies in this business. You never know who's going to be the next executive producer at BET or MTV and is responsible for finding talent.

17. What Are You Thinking

It's never all good

One of the most important things I learned in my life is to think about what I am thinking about when times are not good. Often things go wrong in comedy and in life. The great news is none of that matters. What really matters is what you do next after things don't go right. You can let circumstances take you down or build you up. Protect your thoughts. It's so easy to get in a slump and begin to think negative when life happens. That's so easy that anybody can do it. How hard is it to pick your head up, stick you check your chest out and tell yourself that this will not break you? Very hard! Especially when you've gone through life and it seems like you can't catch a break sometimes. Train your mind to stay positive no matter what. This will take time but it's something that must be worked on daily. Remember "cool head warm feet." Always stay calm and positive and always keep moving. Yes, I had my grandmother who raised me pass away on this journey, yes I had an aunt pass away from cancer three years later and in the midst of everything child support ran my back in court because I wasn't paying enough monthly so now I'm in court trying to convince the judge and state attorney that wasn't in the best situation myself and I do what I can. That's when I learned that the courts don't care about what most men have to say in that courtroom. When I plead my case, my ex-wife go in this envelope and pulls out almost every flyer I was on since January this year. I was impressed mainly because we weren't friends on no social media site, so she went through great measures to get her coins. She still couldn't prove how much money or if was making any money doing comedy. Didn't matter because the judge to me I looked like I'm popular, so I had 3 months to pay a certain amount or I would go to jail. I knew it was ridiculous, but I knew they didn't want to hear what I had to say anyways so I smiled and walked out the courtroom. Soon as I left I talked to God and told him he knows what I'm up against. I had never made that much money in a three month span up until that point doing comedy, but I knew my faith is all that I had so I did what I knew, I prayed and prayed a lot. I knew I couldn't continue doing what I was doing and thinking how I thought so I increased my hustle, faith and prices. I just knew I couldn't go to jail about some money. Long story short God blessed me to come up with the money. I never thought for a second I wouldn't come up with it. I told myself I would every day until it happens. Same thing goes for life. You got to speak life in your own situation. Don't wait for other people to validate your success. Be successful before the world see it. You have to stop trying to convince people that you are worthy of whatever you are seeking and convince yourself. Carry yourself like you are there already. Why not? How do you expect others to see you in a manner that you don't.

I actually believe over the years that society has made us punks. No one wants to get their feelings hurts or hurt anyone else's feelings. For that reason, we have trophies for everyone on the team. My niece's coach tells her cheerleading team that they won the game after every game. That's nonsense. That's not life. Truth be told there are losers. We must have people that lose because that's the only way to determine a winner. We believe these crazy clichés that we were taught growing up which are not always true. People say you can be anything you want if you can just put your mind to it. I believe that this is a big lie. Can I ever be a tree, a fish, the Pope? Probably not. I once seen a video of a little Caucasian girl tell her mom she wanted to be a black rapping police officer when she gets older. Sad part is that her mom never once tells her that it won't happen. We constantly choose being nice over being truthful. The truth is simple as you can be where your talent and abilities can take you if you're willing to put it all on the line and work your butt off. There are several midgets that dream about someday playing in the NBA, will it ever happen probably not.

18.Some Things Must Become an Emergency

It's ok not to be ok, sometimes.

In everything in life there are 3 ways that we look at things. It's either somewhat important, very important or an emergency. When things are just somewhat important to you then you basically take care of it whenever you get a chance too. When it's very important to you it's done a little more often, maybe something with a deadline. When something becomes an emergency, it has to be done right now. You have to make your career/goals an emergency. It can't be put on hold. Not starting today may set you back another 6 months from getting to your goals. You ever received a call that a relative is in the hospital for breaking a leg. Your response may be okay I will go visit them in a few days because it's important but not very important. You ever received a call that a relative was maybe in a car accident, but they are okay. Your response may be ok I will go see them later on after work. It was very important but not an emergency. You ever received a call that a relative had a heart attack or something. You drop everything and stop doing whatever you were doing to get the hospital won't you. Because it was an emergency. You have to work while you are not working. Everyday should be a day of work towards your goals. Michael Jordan was the best basketball player in the world, not in America but in the world but he still went to practice every single day. Even when they didn't have a game he still practiced. Michael made numerous game winning shots in his career, but Mike made those shots days or months before he ever took the real shot. Stay prepared. If you're always ready you never have to get ready. What is your emergency? What are you doing when you are not doing anything? Success doesn't come only when you are onstage in front of crowd with a microphone in your hand. Success comes way before you step on stage. When you have no shows are you still writing? Are you still looking and listening to your set to make it better? Are you promoting yourself to gain more work? Are you studying comedy period or are your social media watching and feeling sorry for yourself because you are not working. Until you make what you are doing an emergency you may not ever get to where you want to be in this business. If you just want to be average, then close the book now and good luck with that but if you truly want to be great then make it an emergency from this day forward. Comedy often have waves. You may be doing shows every weekend for 4 months then 1 or 2 shows for the next 3 months. Your goal should be, to figure out how can I work as much as I choose. I think that if Facebook allows you to have 5,000 friends max on your main page then over half those people should be people that's doing what you are doing or at least in the business. Save majority of fans for your fan page where there is no max friends. You have to know what's going in the business. You can learn what's going on by others in the business. I gain about 70% of my work off social media. I see who's doing things and find out how can I be a part of that in the future. The only difference between you and some of the other comics that are out here doing work and on everything is you are being outworked. It's twenty thousand up and coming comedians that has the exact or similar goals that you do, what will determine if you get to reach yours. All men are created equal, some just work harder when nobody else is watching. You have to position yourself to be successful. Go to those cities where things are happening and build your own name. Yeah it may cost a few dollars but save up, plan a trip for three or four days and hit as many mics as you can. You may live in a cold weather state and need a break from the cold. Plan to go to Los Angeles or Florida during the coldest months to warm up a little and get on some new microphones. It's a win for you. Meet as many comics as you can and make sure they know you when you leave. The easiest way to build your name in another city is to be funny.

19.Commit to Your Commitment

Faith It till You Make It

I learned that no one is more exciting to talk to than a person who's made a decision to do something different. When I first decided I was going to really going to pursue comedy I would tell everyone I spoke too. I was writing jokes about everything I thought could possibly be funny. I was so excited just for a new opportunity. I was committed, so I thought. I quickly learned what real commitment is. Commitment is the willingness to go on long after the feeling from when you first decided to pursue something is gone. December I was excited, January, February I was excited, and the Summer came around and the shows weren't happening like I thought they should be, so I started dusting off my college degree again thinking maybe I should try the workforce again. I wasn't as committed as I thought I were. I was committed as long as things were going great, but no one told me how much work it would actually take to build a name even in the city. I had to go back to the drawing board and figure out a way to stay excited about what I was doing. You have to wake up excited about the journey you're on. It's not going to be easy at all. If it was then everyone will do it. Some comics have mentors that bless them with a lot of knowledge comedy and some of the things they would face during their journey. I never was that fortunate so I learned everything on my own and so I never turn down an opportunity to bless anyone else with what I have learned. The thing I always stress is you have to stay committed. If you're not committed, you won't make it. You have to work towards your goals daily. Even the days you don't feel like it that's when you really should. Make it a habit. Mark Twain said, "20 years from now you will be more disappointed in the things you didn't do." Sometimes you may seem like you aren't getting anywhere. Like you're not progressing and there will be plenty of days like this, keep going. You ever been to the gym for a week straight and at the end of the week it seemed like your muscles are still the same size. To the naked eye on the outside nothing is happening but on the inside your body is preparing itself to grow, keep working you will eventually see the fruits of your labor. If you get up and work towards you craft as much as you can for two, four, five years something has to come from that. It's wonderful to have overall goals but sometimes that can frustrate you a little by looking so far down the road and it seems so far away when that may not be true. I go jogging about a mile a few times a week and when I do I try not to ever look at the end of the mile. I start, and I only look at what's in front of me. The sidewalk blocks that I have to jog over next. I found out that my job is always easier when I deal with what's directly in front of me and when I lift my head up to look at how far I have to go I always get tired quickly. When you start looking at your overall goals you can often get tired and begin to overthink things and try to rush the process. Enjoy the process of becoming. Reaching your goals would be great but the person you become during the process is even greater. You can't be lazy on your pursuit of happiness. I was always taught that laziness leads to poverty. Things of real value or not given away they are earned. Rolls Royce or Maybach are never on sale. You can't get them a at discount ever. You can buy one though, but you've got to earn it. Anything you want in life is very obtainable, but you've got to earn it. You have to be willing to sacrifice things you think you need to hold on too. Sometimes you may even have to cut some relationships with some people. Often the people who you surround yourself with can hold you back. Be mindful of the people you are mostly around. In comedy and in your everyday life. You become like the people you surround yourself with the most. Surround yourself with the type of people you would like to become. Start being professional now. Dress for your success. Show up early. Respect the show whether you are on it or not. Don't be drunk onstage. I remember I was in Atlanta Georgia at the Shaq's next all-star audition at Uptown comedy corner a few year ago. I was so excited because of the opportunity and also, I knew it would be some really good comics on the shows so I would be able to be on a line up with some funny comics. I was so excited that I woke up that morning and the young lady who's couch I slept on started drinking something she had made. It was about 11 a.m. when we started and all day I was drinking and going over material. I was not about to mess this up. It was only 5 minutes, but I made up in my mind to be flawless onstage. drink number 4 then 5. It's 6pm and we have about an hour drive, so we left. On the drive another drink and material, then another. I'm still fine, I'm in my right mind so I'm cool. I get to the venue and I see all the comedians. I'm excited. Most of the comics knew me and I knew them, so we knew the funny was about to happen. Show started, I'm number 7 I think. The host Lavar Walker is getting big laughs one after another. Ok I'm more nervous. I go get a Long Island Ice Tea and drink it before the next comics finished his five-minute set. I'm going over my material. Ok I should change my opener. I tell myself boy sit down you are good. The place is packed, and comedian Shuler King goes right before me and he is destroying the crowd. My first time seeing him and from what I can remember he was hilarious. Now it's my turn. I'm standing on the runway going over my opener over and over. I couldn't hear the crowd anymore I just hear my name called. I go onstage and say my opener, big laugh, then my second joke, laugh. Then all of a sudden I can't remember the rest of my set. This has never happened. How can it when I been studying all day. Now I'm light headed. Am I drunk or something? Then I did something I had never done outside of an open mic. I reached in my back pocket and pulled out my set list right in front of everyone. I read the next few jokes and I heard someone say "boo." I started my next joke and received another big laugh. I forgot my next joke again. I've been onstage 100 times before this. I've performed in front of five thousand people in Miami I'm not nervous past my first joke. I'm drunk. This is not good. Everything was in slow motion at this point. I raised my hand, said my name and walked off stage. I went to the side of the stage where a lot of the comics were wondering why I got off with three minutes left and I just said, "man I'm sick." I got up grabbed my bag and walked out. I heard Lavar making fun of me as I walked out. That's probably the most I've been disappointed in myself. I missed what may have been a great opportunity. When I played arena football between plays I seen Ray Lewis in the stands and I was telling him how I would do his dance after my interception. This when I knew God has a sense of humor. The very next play I dropped an interception that hit me directly in my hands. Ray looked at me and said "opportunities are often squandered by those that don't take them seriously. Stay humble, stay working" Like clockwork the next play I was beat for what ended up being the winning touchdown. He just looked at me and smiled. I felt the same way. I learned my lesson about drinking like that before I perform. I learned everything should be done in moderation. It's not good to be noticeably drunk onstage. Especially when you are trying to make a name for yourself. Shortly after I started getting phone calls and text from different comics. Some just asking what happened and laugh at me for being stupid enough to do something I wouldn't normally do and blow the opportunity. Others were calling me telling me about all the gossiping some comics were doing about me. I didn't mind any of this. I knew I had messed up but like I said earlier comedians talk like high school cheerleaders, so I wasn't surprised, I deserved it. Try not to do anything to tarnish your career. Some people won't let it down ever. I even still hear a story about a particular comedian stealing Eddie Murphy's watch. He later confirmed it was someone else's watch I'm making my point that it happened many years before I even thought about becoming a comedian and people still feel a need to bring it up.

20.Pursue your dream like your life depends on it...because it does

Sometimes you don't need a plan, you just need balls.

Excuses sounds best to the people making them. This is the time to stop making excuses and asking yourself "why me" and start asking yourself "why not me." Be your own celebrity. A big part of your success is not who others think of you but what YOU think of you. What do you want for your life? How great do you want to be? Okay now that you have lied to yourself how hard are you willing to work to be your greatest. Understand in order to be great you will have to be obsessed with whatever you decide to pursue. Anything you want anything you think you may want you can have but it won't come easy. Being great is not that hard anymore because so many people are so good at just being mediocre. This is your life and the only one you will ever get. How will you live it? Motivation is not your problem. Our minds are wired to keep us from the things we fear. Things that are scary, uncomfortable or different. In order to be great, you will have to face them all. I don't like roller coasters at all. I've never been on a roller coaster to even have a fear of them. I don't know not one person that has even been harmed on a rollercoaster. Truth be told many people across the country survive roller coaster rides every single year but in my mind, I think if I get on a roller coaster I will die. I'm not afraid of any haunted house anywhere. Many people are though. I tell myself before I ever enter any haunted house that it's things in there that will purposely try to scare me, but they can't harm me. Therefore, I go in and hear the scary noises and watch the fake zombies jump out and I never once flinch. I made up my mind that roller coasters will kill me, and haunted houses can't so going into a haunted house is easy to me, going on a roller coaster isn't. We often get our secure jobs and go to work because it's comfortable for us. It's an easy win. Taking a chance on our dreams is a scary thing. It's intimidating and uncomfortable and requires more than what we are willing to give sometime. In life we have to sometimes make a decision, are we going to make money or be happy on our way to making money. I often tell people you all may make thousands more than me a year but I'm willing to bet that I'm much happier. It doesn't matter how many times you've failed at trying, you only have to be right once. That one time is the game changer for your life. That game changer moment will never come if you don't ever take chances. Everything around us that makes us happy and miserable is a result of our decisions. You're at that job that makes you miserable because that's your decision. That body that you're unhappy with is that way because you didn't decide to change it yet. That awful relationship you're in is awful because you haven't decided to pack up and leave yet or do the necessary things to make it better. You have to run after what you really truly want in life. Success is never an accident it is very intentional and in your pursuit, you're going to be in the way or on your way. If you don't want it bad, then please step out of the way. I will rather try and never reach my goals than to never try at all. I don't ever want to wake up and wonder what would have happened had I done more with my life. It may not happen in the time frame that you wanted it too but if you quit your dreams will never come true. Get serious about your life, stop talking so much. You've told everybody you know your dreams and you have yet to give 120% every day towards it. I have a brother that had a drug problem. HE would go in and out the hospital every other month seems like. He told the family it was his asthma, but I knew what it was. Asthma may have been included but the drugs was mostly the trigger. We would have all these conversations about it and he would even call me and tell me how he doesn't want to live that life any longer. I tried to feel compassionate, but I knew what the truth was. I knew if he really wanted too he could have shook it, but I never thought that maybe he wasn't as strong as I was. I was thinking on a level of what I would've done. One day he called with the routine and I was as blunt as I ever had been in the past. I simply told him "Shut up! Stop telling people what you want to do and just do it. Get it done. Show us that you are serious and not having a pity party.

Nobody is believing you because we've heard the same stories for years and you've never did what's necessary to get it done." I'm not sure if I hurt his feelings that night but it made me feel good. Stop talking so much. The objective is to be doing good not to just look like you are or want people to think you are.

21. Says Who

GOD is my manager

One thing that I've learned on my journey is that often times you will find yourself frustrated. Things will seem like they aren't going to ever get better. Your final destination seems so far away. You sit and sometimes ask yourself "when will it be my time." You will hear people that haven't made it themselves tell you what you should do to make it. Others will sit around with you and help you throw a pity party for yourself. I've learned to not listen to people. I would rather make my own decisions and live with those decisions whether they work out or not than to listen to someone else and not be sure about my choice. On this journey there are going to tell people that you are not funny enough, you are not using the right material, you're not marketable or you haven't put in enough time. To that I say, "says who?" Bookers won't book you, comics are going to talk about you. You're not excused to be talked down on no matter how cool you may think you are with people. The world is just a cruel place so prepare yourself now for what haven't even happened yet. When people try to attack me I always tell myself that everything and everyone doesn't deserve a response. We have a habit of feeling the need to defend ourselves all the time but some things there's just no need to. The higher up the ladder you go it's going to be people that just don't like you. They will make up lies and try to turn others against you but you must stay on track. Nothing says revenge like massive success. Stay on course. Just because someone says whatever about you doesn't make it true. It's never what people call you it's what you're answering too. If/when the ridicule does start always remember with all the success, all the arenas, theaters and stadiums he's sold out. All the people's lives that he has helped change and all the other good things he's done there are people that still say Kevin Hart is not talented. If he's not, then I would love to see what talent is. What others think about you is none of your business. What other people say about you and your life/career does not have to be your bible. We listen to others just trying to get a little hope about our own situations. Be careful of the information you allow between your 2 ears. I make it my duty to listen to positive things to start my day. Things that will help me stay positive and at peace with myself throughout the day when life starts to weigh down on me. How many times have you heard someone say that someone couldn't do something, and the other person agreed? But why not? Why can't they? Just because someone they look up too says they can't. I've taken on an entire new mentality of simply saying "says who." Everyone attracts exactly what we want every day. Something was ever going good in your life and you thought to yourself that things are so good that something bad is going to happen soon and it did. We often look for things to go bad after so much good or we look for the I knew it would happen moment. We often think no way this can be that easy but why can't it be. It really is that easy. We make things difficult by our thinking. The same way you can bring the bad things in your life is the same way you must bring the good things. Constantly tell yourself a few times daily exactly what you want to happen in your life and then start to work at it. You can hear many people talking but you only listen what's best for your own situation. If you don't have a passion for running your own comedy show, then why even do it. Yes, there are some pros to doing so but there are also many cons. Do what feels good to you but you will not get to where you need to be with work.

22. I've Met Some Cool People

Arrive Unknown, Leave Unforgettable

I can honestly say in my short time doing comedy I've met some really cool celebrity comedians. Not many but the ones I have met I wanted to make it count. I've never been the type of person just to take a picture with comedians that I have never shared the stage with. I have just a few times though because I just admire those particular comics work. First was Patrice O'neal then Sommore. The most memorable comic was Patrice O'neal. I don't remember meeting a lot of comedians and our conversations but with Patrice it was different. I had doing comedy about 2 years, so I would go to the Miami Improv on Tuesday nights sometimes when I had a chance. Patrice was there the following weekend, so I didn't know why he was there so early in the week. All the comics surrounded him as if they were his bodyguards, but he was clearly the biggest in the room. I walked up and stood close behind him as he was telling some story about comedy and everyone was laughing out of control. He finished the story and noticed me standing not far from him. I reached out my hand and in this soft voice introduced myself hoping not to bring attention to myself from all the other comics, "hey Patrice I'm comedian Spunky Robinson." He says "what?" "I'm Spunky Robinson from Miami." "You know there's a comic name Spanky right" " Yes sir Spanky Hayes." "Aye what's your real name?" "Antwon Robinson" "Man use your real name, unless you want to be the next" then he starts naming all these different comedians that used nicknames. I didn't know how to feel about this conversation. He turns to my girlfriend and says, "this you?" "Yeah" "Got damn man she's pretty." Now I'm standing there thinking what the heck man. Good thing she had no idea who he was at this time. We started to walk outside, and he grabs my girlfriend hand and says something I won't repeat, smiles at me and says, "man you do good by this pretty lady and good luck in comedy" then walks off. I don't think I was ever that happy with being disrespected about my girlfriend ever. Later I found out that

that's just who he was. Say what he wanted when he wanted to who he wanted. When he passed away I felt like I lost a friend myself when in actuality our friendship went no further than the ten-minute conversation we had. Rest in heaven Patrice.

My next favorite encounter was with Comedian Sommore. We were at an all-white comedy anniversary event and she wasn't on the show but she came out to support. I was walking out the to sell my merch and when I turned around she was standing right there by herself. I spoke, and she said "oh hey there" like we somehow knew each other. She came towards me and if I can remember correctly she wasn't even walking, it was more like she was floating it was amazing. This woman was gorgeous. No woman has even made me freeze just by looking at her but that's just how beautiful she is. She was dressed in all white that shaped her body so well. I would describe it as being made from God's clouds. I introduced myself and we hugged. I told her I was fairly new to comedy and she just said "well don't stop. It's gone get hard but don't stop." Then she asked do I want to take a picture together. She asked a worker to take the photo, told me it was nice meeting me and walked away. I was so shocked by the entire encounter that I still went out front and forgot my merch. I didn't care though because I just took a picture with Sommore. We all go to the after party and it was a line to take pictures with her. She hadn't even performed but people stood in line for at least 45 minutes just to take a picture. She took a photo with every person that asked. I thought man that has to be tiring. I thought that was so cool that people loved her so much just because she's funny and classy.

23. Make your own moves

I'm everywhere, your never there.

I always hear comedians tell say that they don't know how to put on their own shows on run their own room. Let me be the first to tell you that this won't be easy doing but it's not as hard as some may think. Now before I proceed understand that this does not have to be your bible I'm just telling you how I did things.

If you choose to do it alone first thing is find yourself a venue. A place to have your shows. This is important in a few different ways because location is important. When you find an ideal location ask yourself a few questions. How big do you want your venue? How is the parking? Will your target audience be willing to come to that venue for a show? I say this because I've put on shows in different cities without doing my research and later after a few failed shows that the club had a few shootings and/or vehicle break ins in the past, so the community wouldn't show up. Does the venue sell food and alcohol?

Food is not as important as alcohol believe it or not unless you're running a clean show of course. You can get a venue that don't sell alcohol but then you risk people getting up a few times in the middle of the show to head to the car for a drink. Parking is also important. It's nothing like having 200 cars show up and only 80 parking spots and have people go through a lot of trouble trying to get to your show. Next you have to figure out what type of deal that would like to make with the venue. People put on shows weekly, bi-weekly, monthly or even every other month. It all depends on what you think you can handle. There are some different routes you can take. Choose what will be most beneficial with you and the owners. Understand venue owners don't like to feel like they will lose in any deal. Now that you have a place the next question is who? You can choose to produce actual shows, showcases or just an open mic. Many people run open mics across the country giving back to the city and its comedians. Usually the audience won't pay a fee to come in and watch amateur (for the most part) comedians come and work out their material to hopefully be able to perform it on a paid stage at some point. Most open mics I've been too consisted of mainly the comedians so sometimes you can't really get a good assessment of your jokes. Every now and then in cities like Los Angeles, New York and Chicago you make get lucky and get a true road comic drop in to try out new material because they were in the area. I was in L.A. at the Comedy Store doing a showcase and Martin Lawrence showed up. It happens. Then you have your showcases. They are somewhat like a open mic in most cases but the talent level onstage should be a little better. The audience is usually charged a fee because the comics will usually put on a better show than just at a regular open mic.   Then there is an actual comedy show. That's what I wanted to do. I just didn't feel like I should call anyone out of their bed away from their families for free. People that know me knows that when you see my number in your phone it's one or two things. I'm trying to book you or get booked by you. That's it. A real comedy show has quality comedians that are tried and proven that they can keep an audience attention and keep them laughing. In any show but especially a comedy show that people have paid good money to come see should be ran professionally. No matter how big or small the venue is. The lighting and microphone should be working well. Nothing like watching a funny comic you can't see or every time the comic gets to the punchline the mic goes out. Also, there should be some type of crowd control. We often get hecklers or people who just don't care about what we have to say onstage but don't let that take away from the rest of the audience. If you can't afford security as a host/promoter I always walk over politely kneel down next to them, so I won't bring more attention to them and ask can they please lower their voices or step outside. You must not let it continue because it's people that paid money to actually see a comedy show so do not allow a few rude folks to ruin that experience for them or people won't want to come to another show. I usually say that before I bring the very first comedian on stage. I make it clear.

"Hey look while I'm onstage you all can talk, laugh, shout out or do whatever it is you do but we brought these people here to put on a show and people paid to see a show so please keep your table talk down to a zero. If you don't like the comic, then chill they will be off before you know it or if you just have to have an extended conversation please excuse yourselves. Also, if you have a phone please turn it off or to vibrate. Thank you". That simple. Not mean, not rude just quick and to the point but you must address it. You just do not understand how many people get a thrill out of giving the so-called comedian hell. Also make sure everyone knows how much time they are doing. Make sure they know who's shining the light and where they will be. I've seen a lot of comics cut their time short due to someone taking a picture and they mistakenly thought it was the light to get off stage. A show shouldn't really go more than an hour and a half or two hours tops. If it's a newer comic don't assume they know what the light means exactly. Explain it to them so they fully understand. We all know when the laughs are coming everything else goes out the window.

24. *FACEBOOK, FAMILY, and FUNNY COMICS*

I'm already famous, ya'll just don't know me yet.

What I'm going to address next is all too familiar for a lot of people and it happens more than people actually know. People are sometimes addicted to attention and social media sometimes lead to people to places they should never be in. Some people get on social media almost daily and throw their best jokes or statuses at the world and gauge their likes. They try their best to be funny, positive, or interesting as possible in hopes of gaining attention. The more like they get the more addictive it becomes. How many times have you heard someone talk about how many likes they received on a particular picture or post. Sometimes I've been guilty of it myself. The thing about this is this can often mislead people into thinking they can become a true comedian. This is so far from the truth though. I've been contacted numerous times from people who think they are funny on the internet, so they are funny onstage. Facebook likes don't always transfer in to laughs let me be honest. People be so addicted to the likes that they tend to take other people's statuses to keep the laughs coming. One thing I rarely do is deny people stage time if at my shows it time permits because when I was a young comedian I was denied by the older comics, so I told myself when I got in that position I wouldn't do that to other younger comics. I'm saying that to tell you when I meet these Facebook funny comics and they show up to a show wanting sage time I always ask are you sure. Not that I'm trying to discourage anyone but I know how tough it is up there when all the attention is on you and you can't hide behind your laptop screen or just delete a joke if no one likes it. I can honestly say I have yet to see one do well onstage and not many try it again. Same thing goes for the family funny comic. The person who always starts the party. That person who makes the family laugh anytime they are around. They make their family laugh and their family tells them that they need to be a comedian and they bite the bait. Then they contact other comics and tell them how funny they are. I always tell comics you don't have to make me laugh it's the people out there that needs to laugh. The family funny comic is the worst kind sometimes because they will go onstage with no material and try to be funny in front of strangers not realizing that the audiences doesn't know uncle buck in which most of your laughs with your family comes from. We call it reaching. They are reaching for material in the room to try to get laughs from which rarely works if you're not a seasoned comedian. If you're going to try to make the transition from social media or family funny, then at least try to take it serious. You may not know what you're doing at first but at least have things to talk about

No matter what approach you choose to take please understand that it won't be easy. There's no such thing as an overnight celebrity or fame. Even with the internet. Some of the comics have been shooting those one-minute videos for years before they finally got recognized. Always remember don't compare yourself with anyone else and what they are doing. Try keeping a positive attitude in everything in life no matter what you are aiming at and be consistent no matter what. Consistency and discipline will take you places you will never imagine. Also understand that everyone who's successful at anything always lays a blueprint. You may follow it exactly but study their patterns and how they went about things and work hard. Constantly challenge yourself on your journey. I said it earlier that success doesn't always bring happiness, but progress does. Enjoy the process and all the progressions. Even the small ones.

Made in the USA
Columbia, SC
14 August 2018